# *Home Sweet* KENTUCKY

DAVID DICK

AND

EULALIE C. DICK

WITH A FOREWORD BY BYRON CRAWFORD

First Edition, September 1, 1999

Second Printing October, 1999

Copyright 1999
by
Plum Lick Publishing, Incorporated
1101 Plum Lick Road
Paris, Kentucky 40361-9547

---

Dust jacket design and book production
by Stacey Freibert Design

Dust jacket photograph (front)
by Janet Worne / *Lexington Herald-Leader*

Dust jacket photograph (back )
by Lalie Dick

Photograph of David and Lalie (back flap)
by Chuck Perry

Illustrations by Jackie Larkins

---

## Other books by David Dick

*The View from Plum Lick*
*Follow the Storm*
*Peace at the Center*
*A Conversation with Peter P. Pence*
*The Quiet Kentuckians*
*The Scourges of Heaven*

ISBN: 0-9632886-7-9

Library of Congress Catalog Card Number
99-93121

*For*

Charles Salvador Cumbo

and

Eulalie ("Betty") Harvey Cumbo

Foreword by Byron Crawford
Our Kentucky by David and Lalie Dick

# PART ONE

# PART TWO

# PART *T*HREE

# FOREWORD

Of all the splendid writers who have looked into Kentucky's eyes since Daniel Boone and the long hunters found this place, most have not understood her.

David and Eulalie "Lalie" Dick looked into Kentucky's eyes and saw clear through to her soul.

Kentucky is a beautiful but complex land. The energy hidden beneath her eastern mountains fired America's industrial revolution and warmed a young nation. The timber from her magnificent forests helped build many of America's great buildings, the foremost of which was the humble log cabin in which Abraham Lincoln spent his earliest years. The water from her limestone springs and the bluegrass from her rolling pastures have nourished the finest thoroughbreds ever saddled for the Sport of Kings.

Yet the essence of this good place eludes most journalists because they never really take time to know her–as David and Lalie Dick have done–from the inside out.

David and Lalie have sat with her whittlers and storytellers around her pot-bellied stoves in her old country stores; have meandered down her back roads, rested in her rocking chairs, and visited on her front porches.

David and Lalie have listened to Kentucky's heartbeat and to her whispers and her laughter from Majestic in the east to Madrid Bend in the west. They have read her moods, seen her hidden tears, and understood her dreams.

That is why David's many books, his wonderful essays from Plum Lick in *Kentucky Living*, and Lalie's popular columns in the Kentucky Farm Bureau's newspaper, *All Around Kentucky*, ring as dear and true to most Kentuckians as a grandmother's old dinner bell on a high summer day in the long ago.

"If you really love Kentucky," a woman in the hills once said, "Kentucky will take care of you."

David and Lalie Dick have done Kentucky proud, and the Commonwealth has embraced their work.

We who have read their books and periodic essays have come to admire and love them not only as fine wordsmiths, but as friends and neighbors with whom we could enjoy an afternoon conversation at a corner fence post, across the garden gate, or under a shade tree in the yard.

If all of Kentucky's children were as gifted with the pen as David and Lalie Dick, surely our libraries and our lives would be richer by volumes. But those of us who cannot find words to express our affection for this place must look to such writers as David and Lalie, who have captured many of our own sentiments in the pages of *Home Sweet Kentucky*.

In that sense, their book is really our book–and it lives up to its name from cover to cover.

Beyond their patience and willingness to listen, beyond their compassion and loyalty, David and Lalie also bring to their rich Kentucky essays a perspective of place and spirit.

As a CBS News correspondent who traveled around the world and who walked with presidents, David might have logically been expected to settle down in the Florida Keys or in one of the world's beautiful cities in which David worked. And Lalie, his soulmate, might well have chosen to remain in Latin America, from where she retired as marketing consultant for Revlon International.

Instead, they chose a life at David's ancestral farm home on the headwaters of Plum Lick in Bourbon County, caring for a herd of cattle and a flock of sheep, mending fences, gardening, visiting neighbors, writing, giving talks for the Kentucky Humanities Council, and all the while loving the Commonwealth.

Through their looking glass many of us have seen the reflections of ourselves and our state in a light that gives us pride in calling ourselves Kentuckians.

Whether we are traipsing with David down to the barn on an icy midwinter night during lambing season, or standing with Lalie and her young daughter at the gravesite of renowned Kentucky author Janice Holt Giles, or enduring a drought on Plum Lick, or chatting with eighty-one-year-old Timothy Taylor in the deepest groves of McCreary County, we are able to look right into the soul of Kentucky.

The day David and Lalie came back to live with us was the beginning of a bright chapter in Kentucky's literary history.

*Byron Crawford*

# OUR KENTUCKY

It is not so much "my Kentucky" or "your Kentucky" as it is "our Kentucky." It doesn't belong to the politicians, although they frequently seem to act as if it does. It doesn't belong to the historians. Or the college professors. Or the federal government. Or any foreign government. Not journalists. Not preachers. Not even the poets.

It is the people's home sweet Kentucky–that's the plain and simple truth–unvarnished, lock, stock, and barrel. It is Our Commonwealth. It is our common wealth. It probably doesn't hurt to remind ourselves of the depth and breadth of all this good fortune. We are the heirs of centuries of accumulated treasures, natural and man-made: water and wells, soil and sustenance, air and art. On the other hand, we shouldn't have to bend over backwards to explain this to those who are not native-born Kentuckians.

Before our own passports are confiscated and in order to set the record straight, I, David Barrow Dick, was born at two o'clock in the morning on February 18, 1930, in the Good Samaritan Hospital in Cincinnati, Ohio. My father, who was a young doctor, died when I was eighteen months old. My mother, driving a Model A Ford, moved her young brood back to the place from where she and my father had started their ambitious journey–Bourbon County, Kentucky. I don't feel at fault when I call myself a Kentuckian.

And I, Eulalie ("Lalie") Cumbo Dick, was born at nine o'clock in the morning on March 15, 1945, in the Baptist Hospital in New Orleans. At the age of five my parents, to whom this co-authored book is dedicated, moved to southwestern Mississippi. Theirs too was a journey of sacrifice.

David and I first met at a 1973 Jefferson Davis birthday commemoration beneath the magnolias at Rosemont Plantation in Wilkinson County, Mississippi. Five years later we were married.

In 1985, after David's retirement from CBS and my retirement from Revlon International (I always like to say, "I had this little territory called Latin America"), we moved to Plum Lick, Kentucky, and put down our roots. We returned to the commonwealth where our ancestors–the Crouches, the Dicks, the Grays, the Neals, the Webbs–had lived and loved before us.

Kentuckians seldom see reasons to hoard riches or build walls to seal away natural treasures. There's no surcharge for the beauty of the Commonwealth. The blooming redbuds and dogwoods in the heart of the woodlands don't cost anybody a penny. There's never been a toll on a sunrise or a sunset or a full moon. If there were, we don't know anybody who could afford to pay such a grand token–neither Getty nor Gates nor Rockefeller nor sheik of Arabia. Nor all of them put together.

There are hallmarks that define the place we call Home Sweet Kentucky. It has four seasons–none too severe, none too long, none to unravel our patience. It has capricious mini-seasons when winter seems like spring and summer stoops to autumn. But when we understand and accept the vagaries of nature, then the seasons provide the structure of our lives as completely formed human beings.

While the times of the year furnish the scrim, the actors making their entrances and exits upon the Commonwealth's stage are individual selves. If we cooperate, the seasons mellow our minds, soothe our souls, and work wonders on our unwillingness to let go and allow ourselves to be carried forward to the next natural phase of the year. All good things occur in good time.

Each mold was broken as we Kentuckians were formed. We are rich in differences–diversity gives increased dimension when consummated by a unified people. Each generation represents a new level of the good life: caring and learning, practicing patience, understanding, accomplishing, and forgiving.

It is not boasting to say that each child is destined to surpass her or his parents, affirming that each of us rides on the broadening shoulders of the ancestors who've gone before our allotted time on earth. We've no cause to make fun of the shortcomings of our parents or our grandfathers and grandmothers. We've enough imperfections of our own. Enough to keep us busy doing something about them during our three score and ten. (Or do we now have a better chance for three score and twenty, or thirty, or forty?)

In Ecclesiastes it is written: "...one generation passeth away, and another generation cometh." So be it.

Our "fix't foot"–David's and Lalie's–is Plum Lick, and the describing leg of our compass embraces the Commonwealth stretching from Ashland, Pikeville, and Middlesboro to Paducah, Mayfield, and Hickman. The Kentucky sun widens horizons and clears away misgivings of the night.

The Commonwealth of Kentucky is rightly named. The designation strongly implies togetherness. Unity suggests family ties: church, mosque, synagogue, and always a deeply rooted belief in individualism kindred to Walt Whitman's Song of Myself.

Whatever its structural form, Kentucky is a condition of the heart as well as of the mind, felt with no apologies, thought with an intuitive sense of belonging, measured carefully and fairly with an appreciation for the whole as well as the parts.

We've closed these essays with a "David" or "Lalie" to indicate who was on first and whose turn it was at bat. We acknowledge jointly held creativity and proprietorship. Some essays appear exactly as they were first published, others have been modified to make them more current.

*David Dick*
*Lalie Dick*
*Plum Lick, Kentucky*
*June 3, 1999*

# $\mathcal{P}$ART $\mathcal{O}$NE

*That dog with that outstanding mouth of his hit the
trail, and don't you know he never stopped
until he arrived back on Scrabble Ridge in
Bath County in home sweet Kentucky?*

*And you know what that meant, don't you?
Why it meant he had to swim the Mississippi River.*

# RADIO AND BO

*"If I have a good hound, I run him."*

Kenneth *"Radio"Stewart*
*Scrabble Ridge, Kentucky*

*J*oe Creason is buried by the side of the road at the Longview Cemetery on the edge of Bethel in Bath County. He was laid to rest there in the summer of '74. When passing by, I have a ritual about slowing down and speaking to the memory of the tall, smiling Kentuckian Jesse Stuart called "a goodwill ambassador with a sense of humor who brings sunshine when the day is cloudy."

Usually, it's just a "Hi, Joe," but on special occasions, when in need of a little guidance, I pull over and talk longer to the good man from Marshall County, who gave us *Joe Creason's Kentucky* and *Crossroads and Coffee Trees*. I note the growth of the coffee tree planted directly over Joe's grave. In the new century that tree's going to be really big unless lightning strikes it or some drunken fool runs into it. If anything happens to Joe's tree he'd most likely want it to be replaced. So please remember to do that in case Lalie and I are not here to remind you.

It's about four miles up the road from Joe's coffee tree to the "modern" concrete bridge at Sherburne. In 1975 it upstaged Isaac Kisker's 1868 oak-floored covered bridge, which burned down after two boys built a fire in it to keep warm, they said, on the night of April 6, 1981. This sad event left three covered bridges still standing in Fleming County: Goddard Bridge over Sand Lick Creek, Hillsboro Bridge, and Ringo's Mills Bridge over Fox Creek. This water winds its way to the Licking just south of Sunset.

My neighbor, Michael Hendrix, and I took the road to the right, which is

KY 1324. We poked along, a mile and a half to KY 1602, known locally as East Fork Road. It follows East Fork Flat Creek, which empties into Flat Creek, which joins the Licking behind us at Sherburne. We passed through Pebble, where the road almost touches one of the many loops of the Licking. We made a sharp right and a hard left and climbed up to Scrabble Ridge, where we found, as we were pretty sure we would, "Radio" Stewart.

Kenneth "Radio" Stewart lives with his wife, Mary, in a small house that's seen better times on the edge of Smoky Hollow in Bath County. That's about one mile from the Licking River where Indian Creek empties in. It's downstream from where the Licking twists past Wyoming. (Since there's a Wyoming, Ohio, and a Wyoming, Michigan, as well as several Wyoming counties in the United States, there's no reason why there shouldn't be a Wyoming, Kentucky.) There's no town there now, only the Texas Eastern Gas Company's Owingsville Compressor Station strategically located to give the gas an extra nudge on its way up to New York.

There's no telephone, so there's no way to call ahead. Radio and Mary are most generally at home, along with their fox dogs: Janna, Anna Lois, Patty, Babe, Preacher Man, Howard T., and Image.

Radio Stewart has so many fox hunting trophies–400 to 500–he's taken to giving them away. They're stacked on shelves from the floor to the ceiling in one corner of the front room of his little house, and they're scattered just about everywhere else.

Preacher Man started out being just plain old Son of a Bitch, which was changed to Son of Preacher Man, later shortened to Preacher Man. It could be shortened again to Preach, but so far that has not happened.

Howard T. runs on three legs. He lost one leg in a fence accident. The only way he could get loose was to chew off his right hind leg, which he did. Hardly anything can stop a good fox dog once he picks up the

3

scent. Smart animals know what to do when the chips are down.

Babe was named after "a female I had years ago....She was a good hound," says Radio.

Image reminded Mary of his grandsire, Image. For a while the new dog was called Grandpappy's Image, shortened to Image again, since he was what is known as a "spittin' image." The first Image, who had been first in all his categories, "died of a heart attack right there in the kennel when he was twelve to thirteen years old...went off like slapping your hands together."

Anna Lois was named after a woman in Fleming County.

Joe Creason would have understood the importance of all this.

Radio opened the front door for us and wasted no time taking his favorite chair, where he held forth considerably on his dogs. He doesn't savor coon dogs and other dogs of no consequence. Fox dogs have always mattered most to Radio. He traces his dogs' bloodlines back to Walker foxhounds in Virginia and from there all the way back to England. Somewhere in dog time a really good English hound was crossed with a black and tan, and the rest is fox misery. Radio doesn't kill foxes; the critter is too smart for the dogs and the human beings who run them. The chase is everything. And the chase is enough.

Radio, at age sixty-seven, is about chased out. He's down to six dogs from fifty to sixty. Joe Creason would want to know how Radio got his nickname. Simple. There's a guy named "Radio" somewhere in Nicholas County. Therefore, somebody decided, there should be a "Radio" in Bath County. Kenneth Stewart of Scrabble Ridge was nominated. He accepted and has served admirably ever since.

Then there's the legend of "Bo" (as told to me by Radio). Damn, what a dog.

Bo was in a litter whelped in a Bath County straw stack by a wild dog that had no name. She went out and killed chickens and turkeys to feed her pups. Somebody finally shot her and killed all the pups in the litter except Bo, who defied everybody's dog-killing imaginations. After Bo had grown up enough to know everything he needed to know about the birds and the bees, he was trapped in a barn where some clever, mean-spirited people placed a bitch in heat inside a cage with one way in and no way out.

Bo fell for it. It may have been the only mistake he ever made in his long life. His captors didn't kill Bo. Worse than that. They sold him for a hundred dollars to a man from Texas. Back in the Depression years that was a whole hell of a lot of money. Anyway, the "owner" took Bo out to Texas and one day turned him loose on a hunt. The way it was told to Radio, "Bo was gone, gone, gone." That dog with that outstanding mouth of his hit the trail, and don't you know he never stopped until he arrived back on Scrabble Ridge in Bath County in home sweet Kentucky?

And you know what that meant, don't you? Why it meant he had to swim the Mississippi River. "Took him about six months to a year to sense his way back to his home grounds in Kentucky. Nobody ever captured Bo again."

Nobody ever trapped Bo again in a cage baited with a bitch in heat. Fool Bo once, shame on you; fool Bo twice, shame on Bo.

"He was a big spotted hound...a good-looking hound...marked like a Walker," said Radio, and when a pack of fox dogs got off and running, chances were good that Bo would join the chase. You just knew he was out there doing it, living and hunting and obeying no man for–well, for ten to twelve years.

On the day he died Bo just stretched out on the ground, and he let go.

The way I hear it, after Bo arrived in Heaven, he was chained. St. Peter said, "If we didn't chain him, he'd go home on weekends."

*David*

5

# HEART OF THE MATTER

*T*he geographic center of Kentucky is located near the junction of Cowherd Road and KY 429 near the headwaters of Shepherds Run, Cissels Creek, and Casey Branch in Marion County. Possibly there are purists who'll pinpoint the precise centering somewhere else, and that's all right. Danville and Campbellsville have also staked their claims, to name but two. (My source is C.J. Puetz's County Maps. If this information is not correct, the address is Puetz Place, Lyndon Station, WI 53944.)

On my way down to give a talk in Lebanon, county seat of Marion, I made a special effort to visit the geographic center of Kentucky, a pilgrimage long overdue. I too often stand guilty of thinking that the center of all creation follows me like a puppy after its mother.

Night was falling rapidly, and I decided it was the better part of valor not to go thrashing in haystacks, looking for compass needles. One of these days, I'll go down there and stand on the spot that Mr. Puetz says is the center. I'll probably get help from some of the nice folks I met at the Marion County Public Library, some more of the quiet Kentuckians who are aware of Dr. Laurence J. Peter's "Finster's Law of Location": "Wherever you go, there you are."

Right now and for the time being I'll focus on the idea that I exist for the Commonwealth and not it for me. Individualism is a charming spot on any map, but individualism without regard for community is selfishness by any other name. Ask not what your Commonwealth can do for you but what you can do for it, to borrow from John F. Kennedy's inaugural address. George Bernard Shaw said: "Liberty means responsibility. That is why most men dread it." And Wendell Berry has written "as good a definition of the beloved community as we can hope for: common experience and common effort on a common ground to which one willingly belongs."

NIMBY (Not In My Back Yard) is but one example of selfish disinterest and disdain in and for issues affecting somebody, some-where. John Donne's "No man is an island" describes the responsibility we all share for the common good. The balancing act on the high wire–strong, resolute individu-alism and sensitive, compassionate brother- and sisterhood, played out without a net before a noisy, three-ring circus crowd–requires courage and timing. The imminent danger to us is worth the potential benefit to the community in assembly.

J. LARKINS

There are many preparations for a life of individual responsibility beneath the big community tent. Involvement in our schools and our political system through an open, ongoing dialogue concerning the issues of the day, large and small, will produce a significant difference. NIMBY should be replaced with NIEBY, "Now in Everybody's Back Yard. Talk is usually plentiful and too often cheap, but in the spirit of Kennedy, Shaw, and Berry, each small positive action can make an eventual difference toward the improvement of society. Likewise, each small negative action can lead to the destruction of a splendid Commonwealth within a remarkable nation, a small portion of an irreplaceable planet.

Discussion of issues should lead neither to polarization nor to rancor. Only by talking honestly and unselfishly can we build a better twenty-first century house. The worst payoff will be the one that plunders individualism and drives it deeper into itself; conversely, the best of times will result when exclusiveness becomes inclusiveness.

So, where is the center of Kentucky?

It resides within each heart and mind. But the better resolution occurs with the best of our thoughts and feelings about our collective living in Kentucky.

*David*

# GENIE

*W*hat does a former elementary school librarian do when fourth grade girls ask, "Where are we?"

What does the librarian do when a succession of elementary school girls keep wondering, "How come there's so little mention of women in history books, so few credited with important achievement in Kentucky?"

If you're Eugenia K. "Genie" Potter of Louisville, formerly of Mobile, Alabama, you walk out of the library and spend the next two years compiling a best-selling book, *Kentucky Women: Two Centuries of Indomitable Spirit and Vision.*

From Lucille Parker Wright Markey, whose $5.25 million helped build the Markey Cancer Center at the University of Kentucky, to gold medalist swimmer Mary Terstegge Meagher; from M.A.D.D. activist Janey Fair, mother of one of the victims of the 1988 school bus tragedy in Carroll County, to Claire Louise Caudill, National Country Doctor of the Year in 1994; from African-American artist Elmer Lucille Allen to sculptor Enid Yandell (a good example of the problem with sculptress and other such "– ess" usages)–Eugenia Potter's Kentucky Women is a treasure.

A total of ninety-seven women are included, but the author says, "This book is just the beginning and it is intended to encourage more similar books to be written. Discontinuity among women in Kentucky is not good," she observes, believing that young women today need more role models.

What is the ideal Kentucky woman?

"Depends on the era. The expectations of women have changed. Women can do so many different things now. I hope there'll be more women politicians. I hope for more equal pay, and not so many women working three jobs or in fast foods. Better child care. There's not one stereotype of Kentucky women. I want to overcome that image."

Potter equates "strength in adversity" and "closeness to the earth" with the nurturing of the Commonwealth, as in the case of Judy Martin, who looks "from the mountain with a feeling of protecting the environment and children."

Katherine Pettit, founder of the Hindman Settlement School, was an "educational lamplighter." Ora Porter was the first registered nurse in Bowling Green. When she died at age ninety, a letter to the editor said: "She set an example for many to follow." Ora Porter was another African-American who grew up in a time when "jobs for black women were limited to domestic service."

Susan Pfeiffer is an artist. Audrey Whitlock Peterson was a star basketball player and championship coach. Ruth Mae Geiger fished and hunted and became a professional Lake Cumberland guide. Corinne Ramey Whitehead lobbied in Washington for residents of the Land Between the Lakes. Louisa Woosley was a late-nineteenth-century preacher who warned against women who "bury our talent, or refuse to consecrate all our powers to the work God has given us."

Janice Holt Giles sold more than three million copies of her books, including *The Enduring Hills, The Kentuckians, The Believers,* and *Hannah Fowler.* Mary Edith Engle, pilot, is a charter member of the Kentucky Aviation Hall of Fame. Loretta Lynn soared from Butcher Holler to Nashville and became the first woman to be named Entertainer of the Year by the Academy of Country Music and the Country Music Association. But do you know about the ballads of Sarah Ogan Gunning? She's on page 74 of *Kentucky Women.* Then there's Mary Wheeler, who recorded and preserved "distinctively Kentucky songs." Do you possibly remember Bev Futrell, Karen Jones, and Sue Massek of the Reel World String Band, "the first all-female band since Lily May Ledford and the Coon Creek Girls"?

Mary Desha was one of the founders of the Daughters of the American Revolution. Mary Carson Breckinridge founded the Frontier Nursing Service. Helen Crabtree has spent her life as a trainer of championship American Saddlebred horses. At age eighty-two, she still writes a column for *Saddle* and *Bridle Magazine.*

In writing my own column, "Kentucky Women," I've left out far more than Genie Potter has put into her book by the same name, and she acknowledges that she has omitted more than she wishes. In her Introduction she writes: "Those included are a representative sample, not a comprehensive list. Our libraries are woefully lacking in materials about Kentucky women, and the empty bookshelf will still look curiously blank."

*Lalie*

# FROM ABIGAIL TO ZULA

*J*ust when all those fellas out there thought they had a lock on naming all the dots on the map of Kentucky for every male in the family–from Ajax to Zebulon–along comes a female to say, "T'ain't necessarily so!"

Kentucky's rich community heritage includes not only names of men but names of women who have been responsible for the existence of their communities, crossroads, or settlements–women whose lives made a difference and whose names add a bit of softness to the landscape. In some cases, two or more women's names were combined to put a name on a signpost.

Of course, some liberties have been taken, but if it sounded as if it could be a female's name, I listed it. Faywood in Woodford County or, Rosefork in Wolfe County for examples. Never heard of a woman whose name was Happy? Nelson Rockefeller married one. OK, then what about Butterfly? Well, there was the wonderful actress, Butterfly McQueen, who played the part of Prissy in Gone with the Wind.

I've never seen a list like this before, and by my count there are almost 500 of these wonderful places scattered like stars across the blue of home sweet Kentucky's grasses, hills, and hollers.

Listed by county, here's to you, Ladies!

**Adair**
Bliss
Christine
Columbia
Ella
Eunice
Heraline
Nell
Toria
**Allen**
Clare
**Anderson**
Birdie
Hettie
Sinia
**Barren**
Juanita
Roseville
Tracy
**Bath**
Odessa
Olympia
Olympia Springs
**Bell**
Beverly P.O.
Blanche
Cary
Fonde
Garmeade
Ivy Grove
Murtea
Pearl
Rella
Romona Sta.
Varilla
**Boone**
Caledonia
(Petersburg)

Constance
Florence
Marydale
Verona
**Bourbon**
Elizabeth Sta.
Piper
**Boyd**
Princess
**Boyle**
Aliceton
**Bracken**
Augusta
Gertrude
Parina
**Breathitt**
Daisydell
Lunah
Macedonia
Saldee
Valjean
**Breckinridge**
Rosetta
**Bullitt**
Honesty
Lotus
**Butler**
Dimple
Elfie
Eden
Huldeville
Love
**Caldwell**
Charline
Fredonia
Peach
Ruth

**Calloway**
Cherry
Hazel
Humility
Lynn Grove
Penny
Stella
**Campbell**
Alexandria
Oneonta
**Carroll**
Carson
**Carter**
Charlotte Furnace
Eby
Olive Hill
Rooney
Rosedale
Rose Hill
Sophie
Star
**Casey**
Evona
Joyce
Linnie
**Christian**
Beverly
Gracey
Honey Grove
Kelly
**Clark**
Mina
Tulip
**Clay**
Ammie
Annalee
Benge

Bernice
Dory
Elvira
Eriline
Grace
Jonsee
Oneida
Tinker
Trixie
**Clinton**
Alpha
Ariadne
Desda
Nora
**Crittenden**
Annora
Frances
Irma
Marion
**Cumberland**
Amandaville
Pherba
Leslie
**Daviess**
Livia
**Edmonson**
Lindseyville
Ollie
Prosperity
Rhoda
**Elliott**
Charity
Faye
Lucille
Sarah
**Estill**
Crystal
Patsey

**Fayette**
Loradale
**Fleming**
Elizaville
Marthas Mills
**Floyd**
Alphoretta
Amba
Betsy Layne
Dana
Dema
Emma
Grethel
Ivel
Minnie
**Fulton**
Anne Lynne
**Garrard**
Nina
**Grant**
Delia
**Graves**
Feliciana
Lynnville
Sedalia
Viola
West Viola
**Grayson**
Anneta
Duff
Eveleigh
Meredith
Peonia
**Green**
Eve
Exie
Mell

**Greenup**
Amanda Furnace
Letitia
Lynn
Palmyra
Sunshine
**Hancock**
Roseville (Lyonia)
Victoria Crossroads
**Hardin**
Cecilia
Elizabethtown
Laurel Ridge
Melrose
Sonora
**Harlan**
Alva
Blair
Charlotte Station
Clover
Dione
Louellen
Mary Alice (Beech)
Mary Helen
Pansy (Gulston)
Rosebud
Sunshine
Twila
Verda
**Harrison**
Alberta
Cynthiana
**Hart**
Bonnieville
Eudora
Mount Beulah
Roseburg

**Henderson**
Dixie
Geneva
**Henry**
Glenmary
Lacie
**Hickman**
Beulah
**Hopkins**
Beulah
Jewel City
Vandetta
Veazey
**Jackson**
Annville
Datha
Mummie
Mildred
Waneta
**Jefferson**
Bethany
Lynnview
Maryhill
Medora
South Dixie
**Johnson**
Collista
Elna
Henrietta P.O.
(Chestnut)
Myrtle (Whitehouse)
Thealka
Thelma
Winifred
**Kenton**
Honesty
Latonia Lakes
Visalia

**Knott**
Amelia
Betty
Carrie
Cordia
Dema
Emmalena
Ivis
Mallie
May
Mousie
Nealy
Oma
Pippa Passes
Raven
Tina
**Knox**
Bertha Sta.
**Larue**
Magnolia
Maxine
Tonieville
**Laurel**
Dorthae
Hazel Patch
Ionia
Lida
Lily
Marydell
**Lawrence**
Adeline
Blaine
Charley
Cordell
Ellen
Gladys
Hannah
Henrietta

Hulette
Jean
Jettie
Letonia
Louisa
Madge
Martha
Mattie
Mazie
Overda
Vessie
Zelda
**Lee**
Belle Point
Crystal
Delvinta
Evelyn
Ida May
Primrose
St. Helens
Vada
Williba
Zoe
**Leslie**
Cinda
Essie
Kaliopi
Mozelle
**Letcher**
Arminta
Bilvia
Colly
Cromona
Deane
Eolia
Ermine
Hallie
Kona

Mayking
Polly
Roxana
Tillie
Ulvah
**Lewis**
Hilda
Laurel Point
Rose Hill
Lincoln
Geneva
Maywood
**Livingston**
Burna
Iuka
Joy
Lola
Tiline
**Logan**
Agnes
Dot
Pauline
**Madison**
Estonia
Robinsville
Ruthton
**Magoffin**
Arthurmabel
Bethana
Dale
Edna
Elsie
Fritz
Galdie
Gypsy
Ivyton
Kernie

Lacey (Elm)
Leatha
Netty
Ova
Stella
Tella (Plutarch)
Wonnie
**Marion**
Jessietown
Loretto
St. Mary
**Marshall**
Aurora
Elva
Iola
Melrose
Olive
**Martin**
Beauty
Davella
Inez
Laura
Lovely
**Mason**
Helena Sta.
Minerva
Wedonia
**McCracken**
Camelia
Florence Sta.
(Freemont)
**McCreary**
Beulah Heights
**McLean**
Cleopatra
Faith (Poplar Grove)

**Meade**
Concordia
Rhodelia
Roberta
**Menifee**
Bertis
Mariba
Sudith
**Mercer**
Rose Camp
Rose Hill
Salvisa
Talmage
**Metcalfe**
Peggyville
(Shady Grove)
**Monroe**
Blythe
Otia (McMillan)
**Montgomery**
Hope (Johnson Sta.)
Judy
**Morgan**
Adele
Blaze
Bonny
Elna
Ezel
Floress
Lizzieland
Maytown
Mima
Mize
**Muhlenberg**
Dovey
Luzerne
Lynn City
Sandy

**Nelson**
Lenore
Melody Lake
**Ohio**
Adaburg
Aetnaville
Beda
Friedaland
Magan
Manda
Olaton
Rosine
Taffy
**Owen**
Bethany
Ep
Harmony
Natlee
**Owsley**
Blake
**Pendleton**
Elizabethville
Morgan
Uma
**Perry**
Butterfly
Candy
Daisy
Delphia
(Jewell Ridge Sta.)
Fusonia
Happy
Sonia Sta.
(Butterfly)
**Pike**
Carmen
Chloe
Etty

Goody
Jettie
Jewell
Jonancy
Levisa Junction
(Nelse)
Little Dixie
Meta
Myra (Beefhide)
Myra Sta.
Penny
Phyllis
Regina P.O.
(Marrowbone)
Sharondale
Shelbiana
Virgie
**Powell**
Nada
Rosslyn
**Pulaski**
Albia
Burnetta
Clio
Dabney
Dorena
Nancy
Naomi
Ruth
Ula
Vinnie
**Robertson**
Abigail
**Rockcastle**
Johnetta
Wildie
Willailla

**Rowan**
Christy
Hilda
**Russell**
Catherine
Lula
Old Olga
Olga
Rowena
Rose Crossroads
Vinnie
**Scott**
Alberta
Josephine
Sadieville
**Taylor**
Hibernia
Lorain
Maple
Saloma
**Todd**
Sharon Grove
**Trigg**
Caledonia
Maggie
**Union**
Hazel Bend
**Warren**
Alvaton
Anna
Sally's Rock
**Washington**
Maud
St. Rose
St. Catherine
**Wayne**
Bethesda
Betsey

| | | |
|---|---|---|
| Delta | Dixie | Hazel Green |
| Flossie | Emlyn | Helechawa |
| Susie | Julip | Lexie |
| Zula | Pearl | Mary |
| **Webster** | Polly Camp | Rosefork |
| Oyama | Verne | Valeria |
| Virginia | **Wolfe** | **Woodford** |
| **Whitley** | Bethany | Faywood |
| Clio | Grannie | |

See what I mean by "taking liberties?" I've included a place or two that could have been named for gentlemen whose names were a little feminine-sounding. Rose would be a name like that, but not to mention it on the strength of its having been associated with some of our male friends would be like cutting off the thorns to spite the rose.

There are a few counties, twelve to be exact, in which I found no feminine-sounding appellations, and if your community was left off this list, I accept full responsibility for my magnifying glass malfunctioning whilst I was squinting over 120 old and new county maps. Let us hear from you. We would all love to know where you are!

P.S. If you want to check out a few more details and have a few chuckles along the way, I urge you to pick up a copy of Kentucky author, Robert M. Rennick's *From Red Hot to Monkey's Eyebrow*, or, for a more definitive work, his *Kentucky Place Names*. There's also a wonderful little book called *Guide to the Pronunciation of Kentucky Towns and Cities* by Dr. Niel Plummer. He produced the guide in 1949 and it has been reprinted twice since. I used all three books as a final resource to make sure I hadn't neglected a Happy Butterfly sitting in Maple's shade without a Daisy at Sharon Grove by Betsey Lane on the banks of Melody Lake beneath Mount Beulah.

*Lalie*

# DON'T GIVE UP

*P*lum Lick sits astride the headwaters of the South Fork of the Licking River. It's a blessing to be at the source of such a huge hydrologic system, but a sudden tide can be a curse for all those living downstream. The flood of March, 1997, is a painful reminder of the power of water. It should be a challenge to individuals to understand this natural and inevitable phenomenon.

The Licking is only one of the main rivers in Kentucky that flow into the 981-mile-long Ohio. There are the Big and Little Sandy, the Kentucky and the Little Kentucky, the Barren and the Little Barren, the Laurel and the Rockcastle, the Chaplin and the Dix (formerly, the Dick's), the Red and the Redbird, the Green and the Salt, the Rough and the Rolling Fork, the Mud and the Pond, the Tradewater and the Clark's, the Nolin, the Cumberland and the Tennessee, and the Lost in Mammoth Cave.

There are 13,000 miles of streams and 1,500 square miles of water surface in Kentucky (outlined in C.M. Dupier Jr.'s article on Kentucky rivers in *The Kentucky Encyclopedia*). To ignore or underestimate the power of such a vast system is to invite tragedy. It's too late when national television crews arrive to record the suffering. Lives are forever changed. Property will be restored, but at huge expense.

Living here at the headwaters (little Plum Lick Creek empties into Boone, Boone into Hinkston, Hinkston merging with Stoner to form the South Fork of the Licking River, which joins the main fork at Falmouth), we witness flash floods in their infancies, their temper tantrums. The water level rises and falls in approximately equal periods of time. We recognize it for what is, and we watch it move downstream. We and the cattle, the sheep and the dogs too, stay away from it. We know better than to be trapped by it. We remain on our high ground, yet we remind ourselves about the dangers of being smug.

In March of 1997, the flash flood was greater here than anyone remembered at the time. Plum Lick Creek, which is often between a trickle to bone-dry, looked as wide as a river. No wonder Falmouth was devastated. It received the runoff of hundreds of Plum Licks: Grassy Lick, Mud Lick, Salt Lick, Trough Lick, Indian, Little Indian, Flat, Little Flat, Bald Eagle, Smoky Hollow, Happy Hollow; Aaron's Run, Pretty Run, Strodes, Houston, Harper's, Big Cave Run, Little Cave Run, Peter Cave Run, Slate, Sycamore, and Graveyard Branch. These are only a few of the tributaries in Bourbon, Montgomery, and Bath Counties.

On the banks of each of these tiny veins, in the great arterial system called the Licking River watershed, are the homes of citizens who have the good fortune to have worked together before the flood as well as after it. Everyone can play a part. One of the obvious choices is not to build on a floodplain. It's relatively easy to preach this sermon when you live on the mountaintop or near the headwaters, but the force of water is an indisputable reality. Building on a floodplain, pretending that it doesn't exist, gambling on the outcome, is sometimes an invitation to destruction.

What to do:
- Work together to control the water from the Plum Licks to the Falmouths
- Recognize that impoundments such as Cave Run Lake may result in initial and controversial displacements and relocations, but the greater result is flood control (economic improvement and recreation too)
- Practice diligent soil and water conservation stewardship
- Insist on governmental cooperation (no one person or small group of people can single-handedly build a complex reservoir)
- Remember Murphy's Law–if things can go wrong, they will.

A flood is not evil. It is a natural consequence. We're reminded by C.M. Dupier Jr. that there was a time when today's Ohio River did not exist. During the Ice Age, Kentucky streams flowed into the Teays River in north central Ohio. As the glaciers advanced and then melted, the waters of Kentucky flowed more westerly and the Ohio River was slowly created. Since then, there have been thousands of years of change from Ashland to East Cairo, and uncounted billions of gallons of water have pushed relentlessly to the Mississippi and on to the Gulf of Mexico.

Flood control in the United States has pointed up another reality. Man cannot completely contain or direct the ever-changing passage of Old Man River. Fix here, watch it emerge over there. Also consider the impact on some towns along the way. Hickman, Kentucky, is only one example of a community struggling to survive the meandering of the Mississippi River, which is 2,350 miles long (not counting the Missouri River) and drains an area of 1.2-million square miles. Mark Twain, in *Life on the Mississippi*, has described it as the "crookedest river in the world" with a drainage-basin: "as great as the combined areas of England, Wales, Scotland, Ireland, France, Spain, Portugal, Germany, Austria, Italy, and Turkey.

"If you will throw a long, pliant apple-paring over your shoulder, it will pretty fairly shape itself into an average section of the Mississippi River....The water cuts the alluvial banks of the 'Lower' River into deep horseshoe curves; so deep, indeed, that in some places if you were to get ashore at one extremity of the horseshoe and walk across the neck, half or three quarters of a mile, you could sit down and rest a couple of hours while your steamer was coming around the long elbow, at a speed of ten miles an hour, to take you aboard again."

Such is the challenge facing the engineers and the farmers along the way!

*David*

19

# JEANNE AND TINCY

$\mathcal{P}$enn's Store–where's that located?

Depends on which side of the wood/coal stove you sit and eat your bologna sandwich. I sat in Casey County and Lalie sat in Boyle County 2.2 miles from Gravel Switch, which is in Marion County. (The county line cuts through the center of the store.) Our knees were close to touching even though we were sitting in different counties. This sort of thing has been known to happen, and it sometimes leads to bad jokes.

Nestled up close to the North Rolling Fork River, for 150 years Penn's Store has been a favorite meeting spot for just plain folks, although tourists lately have been trooping in from as far away as Australia, Russia, China, Japan, England, and Ireland. Must be something special about the place– "The Oldest Country Store in America in Continuous Ownership-Operation by the Same Family."

First of all, there are the owners, Jeanne and her eighty-one-year-old mama, Alma Penn "Tincy" (pronounced Tine-see) Lane. People don't get any more home sweet Kentucky than Jeanne and Tincy.

Then there's the famous privy–Penn's Privy–about as nice a common denominator as you'd want to see this side of the Taj Mahal or the throne of King Whatever. Chet Atkins and Billy Edd Wheeler dedicated the outhouse in 1992, and each October there's an "Outhouse Race at Penn" Store, a 500-foot single elimination in heats of two. The first, second, and third prizes are outhouse miniatures.

Penn's Privy has become so celebrated that Tincy and Jeanne have had to lock it the way they do at some of those fancy places out on the interstate. But out there in the fast-lane facilities you won't likely find a nice vase of dried flowers, individual scoops of lime, and a seat as smooth as a poplar limb.

Clemens Caldwell stopped by for a chat. Named for Samuel Clemens (Mark Twain), Mr. Caldwell is such a regular Wednesday feller, you'd probably not figure it out that he owns land and bank stock. Clemens likes to talk about his parrot, R.C., his prize game hen, the late Minnie Myrtle, and the orphan sparrow (don't suppose it has a name), who all live in the house with Mrs. Caldwell. Minnie Myrtle used to peck at the back door, then come inside to lay her daily egg.

"A whistling woman and a crowing hen never come to any good end," according to Clemens, an idea that may scale the heights of political incorrectness, but he claims it's 99.9 percent true, and we didn't see any immediate reason to argue with him about it.

Cousin Hazel Roberts and her daughter, Georgia, came in to sit a spell. Hazel will be one hundred years old on August 11, 1999. Earlier this year she fell and broke her pelvis. Georgia is learning to walk with her new artificial leg, but it hasn't affected her organ playing at the Baptist Church in Mitchellsburg, Kentucky. She'll be seventy-five years old in October of 1999.

We applauded when Jeanne's twin daughters, Dava and Dawn, sang two sweet songs, "If You Love Me, Really Love Me" and "Coming Home to You." Born nine minutes apart and singing together since they were eleven years old, Dava and Dawn have grown up to be beautiful women to behold and just as beautiful to hear. They performed at the1996 Kentucky State Fair. They say they're shooting higher than the Grand Ole Opry.

"Just because we're from Gravel Switch doesn't mean we only do 'Hee-Haw,' although there's nothing wrong with 'Hee-Haw,'" said Jeanne Penn Lane from behind the counter where she and Tincy waited on local customers.

"Peg" Johnson opened the door and with his crutch swinging as reliably as a divining rod, went directly for a soda in the front cooler. Peg said

21

he lost his right leg after a tree fell on him when he was a boy. He seemed as contented as anybody did with two legs.

Roger McQueen (distantly related, he said, to the late Steve McQueen, the tough guy in old movies) made a call for a sausage company. Tincy studied the situation for a minute and decided to order three packs of ham and cheese. Roger brought in the order, then went on making the rounds of the Knobs country.

Penn's Store used to include the post office. The first postmark was "Rollings, Kentucky, November 7, 1882." Today the space that was the post office holds herbal things grown in a little outside garden. For some folks that's a good sight better than junk mail. The "Herbal Harvest" has been an annual event here, and with any kind of luck we'll be there. "Wood Stock" has been another event, which Jeanne likes to call "a celebration of wood by wood artisans, wood business, and forestry."

"Country Store Christmas" has been held in late November and early December. Who knows? After you've walked all those malls, you might want to stop by Penn's Store and rest a few moments.

*David*

# MARY DEE

$\mathcal{S}$o how does a woman grow up to become the manager of one of Kentucky's fifty-one state parks, facilities that are the envy of every state in the union? She begins by having a natural love of the outdoors, and she laughs, "I kinda slipped into it."

She's Mary Dee Miller, "Dee Dee" to her brothers and her sister, "Mary Dee" to the staff at the John James Audubon State Park in Henderson, Kentucky. As manager she's responsible for seventeen employees, including three park rangers, a priceless museum dedicated to legendary American ornithologist and artist John James Audubon, and 682 acres of natural forest, that includes a golf course and is home to thirty-five species of warblers.

Mary Dee is also mother of soon-to-be-nine-years-old Scottie Maria and seven-year-old John, better known as Jack. Unlike her brothers, she's not a hunter. She cares about the nature of things, but it's been a long trail winding from waitressing after high school and two years at the University of Kentucky before dropping out. Mary Dee's father, J.R. Miller, moved to western Kentucky from Vicksburg, Mississippi, in the late '30s. He started Big Rivers Electric Cooperative and was manager of Green River Electric until his retirement in the '80s. He became chairman of the Democratic Party in Kentucky, but his daughter sought a different direction.

"I was not interested in politics at all," Mary Dee says with a shake of her head. "I really wanted to go into zookeeping...I went to Washington to visit my sister and she took me to the zoo...I'm not a city person...I wound up coming back to Kentucky, packing up and moving to Florida to study biological parks and zookeeping."

She received an associate degree from Santa Fe Community College, then came back to Brescia College in Owensboro, Kentucky, to study elementary education in order to teach others about things natural.

23

Mary Dee Miller became a naturalist at Lake Barkley State Park and from there she moved to Barren River State Park, where for seven years she was the Park Naturalist. Up and down the nature trails she led adults and their children. In her continuing quest for knowledge to share, she enrolled in folklore and museum classes at Western Kentucky University. But there are, as they say, only so many hours in the day and something had to give. "I was working every day, most all weekends, and going to school," she says.

Her interest in museums meshed perfectly with Audubon State Park, and when the manager's position became available in 1986, she moved into it. "The opportunity here is so different from resort and [the usual] recreational parks and historic sites," says Mary Dee, who is more interested in the warbler population and the wetlands acquisition that she is in hotel and motel management.

Ironically, there is no financial assistance from the National Audubon Society, but a loyal support group known as the Friends of Audubon tries to offset whatever deficits there are. Several years ago, when the Friends could see the acquisition of a fabulous collection of Audubon's works slip through Kentucky's fingers, a dedicated group of volunteers knocked on doors in neighborhoods and corporations to try and keep the collection in Henderson.

"Even elementary school children sold calendars and drew pictures of birds," says Mary Dee. "They created their own museum and charged admission to raise money. There were even people who gave a dollar and said, 'I can't give any more, but I want to give something.' We now have the largest collection of the quadrupeds, the mammals Audubon drew after he drew *Birds of America*," says Mary Dee proudly. Some of that collection includes Audubon's memorabilia–the oil painting of the Bald Eagle that hung above the fireplaces of the Audubon family homes, the gift of buckskins to Audubon, and the bronze bust of Audubon that has its face from the life mask.

Although Audubon State Park is off the beaten track of Highway 41 in Henderson and is not considered a final destination, approximately 17,000 patrons from all over the world each year pay to visit the Audubon Museum.

Each October the Big River Arts and Crafts Festival is held at Audubon Park, attracting about 200-250 vendors and 50,000 visitors.

You would think that with that many people strolling back and forth eating funnel cakes and drinking coffee, there'd be the typical fall festival trash problem–but not at Audubon. Mary Dee and her crew zoom in on stray cups and discarded napkins like wood ducks on wooly worms.

What is the future for this priceless place? "We need to educate the public. We need to think more about the environment. We need to get back to the history of Kentucky, purchase land to expand 'green spots,' and become enforcers of the [public] property."

One way to help preserve Kentucky is to purchase one of the Kentucky environmental license plates for an additional $25–either the cardinal or the Kentucky warbler. "Most of this additional money goes into a fund for the purchase of green lands in Kentucky," says Mary Dee. In the meantime, Mary Dee and Friends are doing their parts to help keep the Audubon legacy alive for our children and our children's children in home sweet Kentucky.

*Lalie*

# MRS. WALLIS

"*S*he had one child in her marriage and I believe the child lived one week, and she never had any other children," said Judy Ferrell, softly, from her seat at the large dining room table in the stately Nannine Clay Wallis Home in Paris, Kentucky.

"Children were very important in her life even though she didn't have any...she allowed all of the children to come and play in this yard. They were always welcome."

On a frigid Friday in early February, Judy Ferrell, long-time garden club member, now chairwoman of the State Garden Club Headquarters and Arboretum, told the story of a piece of Kentucky that can best be described as a one-of-a-kind gem worth nurturing. Sitting in these friendly surroundings, listening to Judy recall the history of a lovely place, it seemed as if outside the frosted windows, under the sod of the frozen surface of the big yard and under the bare, winter-gray branches of the trees, there was life waiting to burst into spring.

Native Bourbon Countian Nannine Clay Wallis, born in 1881, educated in Kentucky, Maryland, and New York, married Frederick Albert Wallis in 1901. In 1925, Mrs. Wallis inherited from her father, Thomas Henry Clay, the stately home and seven acres on Pleasant Street in Paris. She shared his love of gardening and flowers, and their love of flowers and gardens became their legacy.

Upon her death in 1970, she left her family's residence and gardens to the Garden Club of Kentucky, with the provision that the home would be its headquarters for thirty years. Now, twenty-five years later, Mrs. Wallis would probably be pleased to see her love of children and education flourishing as only she could have envisioned.

"All of a sudden, the Garden Clubs of Kentucky had this magnificent property and a wealth of trees and...a landscape architect said, 'My goodness! This is a mini-arboretum...this is just something fantastic.'

"The wheels began to turn and...and we said, 'the lady's love was education and children...her beautiful gardens and her home, which she wanted us to have...we'll turn it into a public arboretum!'"

Judy explains that an arboretum is an outdoor classroom in which a collection of different trees and shrubs is cultivated for scientific or educational purposes. "This is exactly what we did and what we are doing: the Nannine Clay Wallis Arboretum was dedicated April 3, 1992."

Students are given a free study guide; a small contribution is requested from non-students. "We've had students and their teachers and professors come from all over Kentucky. Some children come to study on their own so they can apply for special projects or awards in their schools."

A professional video is in production with a grant from the Kentucky Division of Forestry. "It will show the arboretum in each of the four seasons and, of course, it has children in it. So when students come here, we will bring them in, show the video, whet their appetites, give them their study guides, and take them out and let them have fun!"

The study guide includes a map and a key. Each tree in the arboretum has something written about it, a drawing of its shape or its fruit. "The children get out there and they have the best time and say, 'Oh, I'm going to find this!' or they find the leaf, then they find the tree. They read the signs that tell what it is and they laugh...It really becomes so exciting!"

Grants and matching funds are important to the Wallis Home and Arboretum. Matching funds come from the Garden Club of Kentucky or in-kind service–all contributions are strictly voluntary. Women (some men too) come to the arboretum from all parts of the Commonwealth to work in the various gardens or just to pull weeds, each slip of green counting as a labor of in-kind love.

More than two thousand Garden Club of Kentucky members from each county in the state comprise five districts: "Many ladies...take on projects here–the TV was bought by the Dogwood District, the butterfly garden...was done by the Limestone group. The Audubon district is...funding the cabinet for the TV and VCR, the Blue Grass District restored the martin houses that were on the property, and the Mountain Laurel District did some of the restoration of the pigeon house that was found in the carriage house."

A public Arbor Day celebration was held in April of 1995. New trees in the arboretum were dedicated. A new conifer garden has been on the drawing board, and there are plans for an intern to help bring back to life one of the silent, overgrown gardens.

Mrs. Nannine Clay Wallis's love of children and education is being cultivated and nurtured–blooming with the help of thousands of hands across the commonwealth.

*Lalie*

# BUCKHORN LAKE

$\mathcal{S}$cotland's Loch Ness, with or without its doubtful monster, can't claim one speck of superiority over Kentucky's Buckhorn Lake.

Located on the Middle Fork of the Kentucky River in Leslie and Perry counties, Buckhorn is a jewel set in a crown curving through the Cumberland Plateau. There may be a bobcat or two, a rattlesnake or two, but their realities can be adjudicated (legal language for giving wide berth to or steering clear of).

In late summer, I received a call from one of the organizers of the annual Combs Family Reunion, held at Buckhorn Lake Resort Park and having not a thing to do with bobcats or rattlesnakes.

Their scheduled speaker couldn't be there, so would I come up and give a little talk? I considered it a high honor and felt blessed that the weekend was open. We'd been talking about going somewhere to get away from the varmints of the regular workaday world.

The drive up the Bert T. Combs Mountain Parkway was as splendid as it always is, no matter the season. We headed south from Campton and worked our way past Jackson down to Chavies and over to Buckhorn Lake.

It was nothing like stepping off the train at Inverness, Scotland, and being met by a silly person in a green monster's suit. It is a comfort to know that Buckhorn will never have to resort to such clowning.

You can sit on your own little porch at the lodge and watch the sun go

J. LARKINS

down as beautifully as anywhere on the face of the earth, Scotland included. At daybreak, you'll be a witness to creation.

On that Sunday morning we joined a small group of Combs family members and drove up and down the winding road to the Log Cathedral at the Buckhorn community. You just have to see it to appreciate it.

The church's simplicity soars.

Completed in 1928, the inspiration of Harvey Murdock of Brooklyn, New York, the Log Cathedral reminds me somewhat of a giant ark that's come to rest against a mountain slope. From the vantagepoint of the pews, the organ (restored after a devastating flood) now seems thrust up high enough to reach all the way to the Pearly Gates.

The First Annual Combs Family Church Service dates back to 1990 (that was the morning of the Twenty-eighth Combs Family Reunion), and Brad Napier is remembered as having commented on the organ:

"It is a ten-rank Hook and Hastings tracker-action organ that is now electrically powered. But many years ago, down in the room below the organ, there were boys that pumped bellows to force air into the pipes to make the organ work, and I have heard it told that the organist at the time would have to kick and bang on the bottom of the organ because the boys would fall asleep during the sermon and wouldn't waken for the last hymn."

The organ was destroyed in the flood of 1957, along with the pews and anything that looked like a hymn book, a reminder that the days of old Jonah aren't always so long ago and far away.

Construction of Buckhorn Lake began in 1956, not in time to save the old organ in The Log Cathedral, but work on the impoundment was completed in 1961 at an original cost of under $12 million. It's estimated that since that time the Corps of Engineers project has prevented more than $38 million in flood damages, and maybe it has saved an organ or two. Possibly, also a choir member or two.

I spoke with one of the survivors of that time at this year's Combs Family Reunion. Her name is Virginia Harris Combs. She's ninety-seven and a half years old.

What Miss Virginia told me about her failing sight and hearing is a piece of wisdom I never brought back from any Loch Ness. It came straight from the heart of Buckhorn Lake in home sweet Kentucky:

"My eyes and ears are in Heaven, waiting for the rest of me."

*David*

# TRAIL OF THE LONESOME PINE

*T*he Bert T. Combs Mountain Parkway through Clark, Powell, Wolfe, and Magoffin counties in October is like a taste of vintage honey. The spectacular autumn disclosure is about to happen. The drive past Salyersville, Prestonsburg, and Betsy Layne to Pikeville puts you deep into some of the best scenery Kentucky has to offer. The Daniel Boone National Forest with its Natural Bridge, and Jenny Wiley State Park are examples of what good conservation can do for society.

U.S. 23 from Prestonsburg to Pikeville is a good example of how to mess up a good thing. Development is one matter: helter-skelter development is another. One man's honey is another man's hodgepodge. It's also true that land suitable for development along the U.S. 23 corridor is scarce and comes at a considerable premium. Its very nature presents a challenge to achieve the delicate balance necessary for the preservation of anything remotely resembling the original beauty.

This stretch of road is no isolated example–similar scenarios exist throughout the Commonwealth and the nation. Accommodations have to be made and compromises are inevitable, but the idea that "anything goes" in the development of God-given land for the debatable benefit of a burgeoning population is selfish and self-destructing. All of this is subjective judgment. Beauty is in the eye of the beholder. It can't be legislated; but it can be influenced. If music appreciation can be taught, why not countryside appreciation? Do we have to settle for an environment that is gobbled up with another hundred or more franchises?

If this is our fate, why can't there be more beautification efforts by civic organizations as well as individuals? If anyone thinks this is a case of overreaction or kooky activism, make the drive from almost any Central or South American or Caribbean island airport into the city it serves; ask if this is how Kentucky should look. There's neither simple answer nor quick fix. Pride in the territory comes with the territory. The remedy begins at home with the individual. Too often the individual left to her or his own devices will drift unerringly in the direction of discord.

It takes planning. That's what caused there to be a Daniel Boone National Forest and a Jenny Wiley State Park and a Mountain Parkway to connect them and make them more accessible to other parts of the Commonwealth. Without the planning and the commitment to excellence there well might have been another exercise in selfishness.

It takes control. Littering has to carry enforceable penalties; otherwise the tendency frequently is to think that throwing something on the ground implies there's a lower social stratum to pick it up.

It takes vision. One man's vision is another man's blind spot. We don't all see alike, yet there should be more meeting places where we can send elected representatives to point to the future and decide more clearly what is best for the many as well as the few.

It takes understanding. Some things destroyed cannot be replaced in millions of years, much less within a lifetime: the Grand Canyon; the Great Lakes; the Great Plains; the Red River Gorge; the Kentucky River palisades. Our own front yards and our own back yards are equally precious. This may contradict an increasingly disposable society in which we treat almost everything with tissue paper disregard, but contradictions by their nature are challenges for planners, comptrollers, visionaries, and the wise.

Soon the magnificent road from Winchester to Clay City, Stanton, Slade, Campton, Helechawa, and Salyersville will be in its ultimate autumn splendor. The leaves will be in their triumphant reds and softer yellows, while the pines and cedars remain ever green. God help us if the day comes when the parent trees are uprooted in the name of progress and in their place is poured another slab of concrete where might be bought a faster hamburger or a sexier videotape.

*David*

# SARA

*S*he loves to talk on the telephone.

She loves to talk on the telephone with the receiver nestled between her right ear and shoulder as she hurries from the living room through the dining room to the kitchen, down to the basement and back to the kitchen again.

She loves to talk on the telephone as she rushes across the state in her automobile, usually accompanied by her faithful companion, Rusty Red Dog, a golden retriever.

She admits it: she's a workaholic.

"This campaign clearly established me on my own," says Sara Walter Combs, elected November 8, 1994, with 70 percent of the vote, to the Kentucky Court of Appeals, 7th District, 1st Division.

Although her official office is located in Stanton in Powell County, Sara's responsibilities extend across the Commonwealth. The young widow of Governor Bert T. Combs is as much at home in Frankfort and Louisville (where she was born and bred) as she is on Lower Cane Creek in Powell County, where she continues to live with three dogs, two cats, and a pasture full of miniature horses. Sara and the late governor named their farm Fern Hill, the title of a Dylan Thomas poem.

The first woman to serve on the Kentucky Supreme Court, Sara Walter Combs was defeated by Janet Stumbo in a regular election for the high court. Sara was then appointed to the Court of Appeals seat vacated by Judge Stumbo, and in the subsequent election, Sara emerged victorious. Even though she campaigned on her own name and her own record, she has not forgotten the central love of her life, the late governor. "He will walk with me all the days of my life...He will always be the person who helped mold me," said Judge Sara Combs the week after Thanksgiving on Fern Hill.

To watch her order everybody else out of the kitchen while she washes the dishes–polishes the bottoms of the pans in which she has cooked another gourmet meal (she really knows how to do a "Hot Brown," making every other one seem like so much ham and turkey drowning in cheese), cleans up the counter space the twelfth time with a damp cloth in sweeping circles like radar looking for the smallest flecks of food–to watch this, is to understand the boundless energy surging from this tiny person.

She puts away her shoes when she's at home in her cabin, and she treats her visitors as if they are the most important people in the world.

Judge Combs sees the Appeals Court as "...essentially the tool of the people, not some entity in isolation. It's an intermediate court and, as a practical matter, it is the average person's last resort to justice. Everyone is entitled to one appeal. It's a matter of right. The court is responsible to needs...The role of the court is to point out discrepancies," says the judge, recalling Victor Hugo's Jean Valjean, who spent twenty years in jail for stealing a loaf of bread.

Although the discrepancies of 1994 may never be that grave, Judge Combs wants to help insure that everyone is entitled to that one appeal, whether it be workers' compensation, domestic relations, criminal matters, contract cases, or tort cases.

Sara Combs views public service as a requisite individual responsibility for the general good of the community. She often refers to President John F. Kennedy's use of classical references, as in Pericles from ancient Athens: "Every individual had a role to play. We say here that a man who is not interested in politics is not minding his own business."

A student all her life, Judge Combs is not resting on the laurels of her convincing election to the Kentucky Court of Appeals. "I want to continue to learn and hone my skills, learn other languages [she's been a teacher of French, Spanish, and political science] and re-study the classics."

Sara Walter Combs is still adjusting to the loss of her husband on December 3, 1991, when floodwaters of the Red River swept him away. After his body was recovered and was buried in the hillside cemetery along Beech Creek in Clay County, Sara's close friends urged her to sell Fern Hill, but she refused to do it.

"There's a gnawing loneliness that never leaves," she admits, but in her own right, the new judge is committed to the preservation of Fern Hill. She says she cannot imagine leaving it.

When Judge Sara Walker Combs is not writing opinions for the Court of Appeals, not talking on the telephone at home or out on the highway, not giving talks at schools and service organizations all over the Commonwealth, not cooking gourmet meals for visitors, not filing the papers of her late husband, not tending his rose garden, she often relaxes by hanging wallpaper.

Judge Combs's prescription for hanging wallpaper could apply to almost any line of work in life: "Match the pattern, make sure there's enough glue, and smooth out all the lumps."

*Lalie*

# Ms. Hatmaker

$\mathcal{S}$he's a doer's doer. She's a mountain woman's mountain woman.

She's Louise Hatmaker, and she's accomplished enough in one lifetime to add up to several and then some. She doesn't go anywhere for very long these days. Louise Bolton Hatmaker stays as close as possible to Perry County where she was born and Breathitt County where, until two years ago, she was publisher of the two oldest newspapers in the Kentucky River Valley–*The Jackson Times* and *The Beattyville Enterprise*.

"I've always been proud of my mountain heritage," said Louise after she received this year's "Combs of the Year Award" at the 36th Combs Family Reunion at Buckhorn Lake State Park. She traces back through her mountain mama, Zada Baker Combs Bolton, to John Combs, an Englishman who came over on the Magnolia, landing at Jamestown in 1619. Six generations of Combses have claimed Eastern Kentucky as home since another John Combs was born in 1735. The clan has produced such notables as the late Governor Bert T. Combs, for whom the Mountain Parkway is named, and the immortal Earl Combs, who played the outfield for the New York Yankees and had a twelve-year batting average of .325.

"You notice most of the names [in the chart of the Combs family] are men," said Louise, who certainly has proved that mountain women have knocked their share of home runs. I first met Louise when I was competing with her at the Kentucky Press Association. Well, maybe we weren't competing. We were two women getting to know each other, and we were laying the groundwork for mutual respect.

"Keep a good attitude and don't go around worrying," was Louise's answer when I asked her for advice for young and older Kentucky women today. "I don't do things for the credit, I do things because they need to be done," she added with a smile. "If you get an opportunity to better yourself, take it."

In her "retirement," Louise Hatmaker recalled the editorial policy of her newspapers: "You need to do something good for your town. You can print the bad but print some good things too."

Louise lost her twelve-year-old son in 1964. As a result of that experience she became committed to the education of retarded children. She believes that "God puts children with mental and physical handicaps on earth for us to learn from them."

Louise Hatmaker's honors are legendary. The Kentucky Press Association named her recipient of the Russ Metz Most Valuable Member Award for 1997. She has been a member of the KPA Board of Directors for more than twenty-two years. She was the first woman president of the Natural Bridge Park Association and is an honorary General in the Kentucky National Guard. She and the late Gov. Bert T. Combs are the only two recipients of the Eugene H. Combs Humanitarian Award presented by the Combs Family Association.

Now in a battle with cancer, Louise Hatmaker is, as you would expect, being positive. "No hang dog look," she says, "I've been very open about it." After surgery she underwent radiation and chemotherapy. When she walked in the first time, she said, everybody looked sad. "It looked like a morgue," so, she said, she began to laugh and joke. Her doctor said, "Louise, your attitude is so good, you've helped not only the patients, doctors, and nurses, [you've helped] yourself."

It's fair to say that I like that idea and maybe it'll work for Kentucky women, whether or not they're descended from John Combs. It's called, in Louise's words, "Women not taking the back seat, being leaders in [any] field."

Certainly, there's nothing wrong with taking the back seat if that's your choice, but women don't have to be relegated to it the way they used to be. When I left her there at Buckhorn, Louise Hatmaker was generous with her time, and she had a big smile on her face. "If you have half as much fun in your newspaper career as I did in mine, you'll have a wonderful life."

When I think about the big metropolitan newspapers, the flashy newsmagazines, and the powerful network television news programs, I begin to wonder if it might not be to their and the country's advantage if they climbed down from their high hills and visited the real mountains of Kentucky. They may be so fortunate as to find a Louise Hatmaker, and we may all be so fortunate if they listen to her wisdom and put some of it to work.

*Lalie*

# J.R.

*T*he Bluegrass Parkway was quiet. Night had settled in. Soon it would be midnight. The Kentucky River lay ahead. It slipped through its silent palisades as it has for hundreds of millions of years.

The tires of the 1997 westbound traffic were humming with rushes of wind sandwiched between big trucks gaining momentum; it was as impersonal as it was hurried, desperate for competing destinations. There was no pervading "road rage," but neither was there any imperative for being kind and possibly helpful.

It was a time for reflection about that morning's encouraging meeting with the University Press's acquisition editor for my first historical novel, *The Scourges of Heaven*, about the cholera epidemics of the 19th century in Kentucky. We were hardly thinking now of any other kind of scourge.

"What was that?" I blurted to my better half, who was driving at the 65-mile-an-hour speed limit.

The sound was like a witch's knuckle popping. Or maybe it was a tree limb snapping where a tree had no reason to be.

"I don't know," she replied, both our faces staring straight ahead into the darkness. At that precise moment, she was in the passing lane.

Quickly, there was the sound of many witches' knuckles popping in a forest of limbs snapping, where no forest had any reason to stand. My wife's own knuckles tightened on the steering wheel, and she calmly guided the car to the outside lane and finally onto the generous shoulder.

Blowout.

Most folks have had their blowouts and each one is a different experience. For a few seconds we sat in quiet gratitude that we had not been coming down the hill to the Kentucky River. We had not been passing a semi or a double-hitched rig or a recreational vehicle headed for Florida. It was not raining. Not snowing. Not icing over. It was, so far, the best kind of blowout.

The jack was in the trunk where it should have been. It would have been better if it had not been at the bottom of boxes of books, *The View from Plum Lick, Follow the Storm,* and *Peace at the Center.* At this eleventh hour the view was dark, a storm was always a prospect, and there was no certain peace at the center.

We unloaded the trunk and piled the boxes by the side of the road. I positioned the jack under the car's chassis on the parkway side where inches separated me from whining 65-mile-an-hour eighteen-wheelers. The faces of human drivers were as invisible as they were indifferent. I felt as innocent and helpless as a well-intended woolly worm about to be mashed to smithereens.

I raised the car a tiny bit and figured it was time to loosen the lug nuts. I could not remove the wheel cover, which was probably a good thing because by the time I might have changed the tire I would have been in woolly worm heaven predicting weather for angels.

My wife walked up the road to determine the mile marker (65) and returned to the car to call for help on the cellular phone. When the tow truck arrived from Carey's in Lawrenceburg, we met "J.R." It sure is comforting to know that there are some good-as-gold, honest-dealing, unselfish, courageous "J.R.s" in the world.

This one lay on his stomach by the side of the road, jacked up the car, changed the tire, announced that he didn't trust the little, poor-excuse spare, told us to follow him across the Kentucky River, and led us to the garage on the Lawrenceburg side of Stringtown. At midnight he prowled through the junkyard like a friendly dog wanting to share a bone.

He came out with a tire with plenty of tread, removed the manufacturer's spare, and replaced it with something he called "better than it was before."

"How much do we owe you for the replacement?"

"Not a thing."

Of such senseless acts of kindness are human beings bonded.

I went to the trunk and took out a copy of *The View from Plum Lick* and inscribed it "To 'J.R.,' (Clell Evans, Jr.) with thanks for bringing us in safely from the parkway."

As we headed west toward Elizabethtown to grab a few hours of sleep (our daughter and a dog and a blown-out tire piled high in the back seat), we felt better about individuals living and working and caring about other individuals. If we'd been murdered at midnight in the darkness where the river cuts through, we would have been big news on the next morning's television program.

Instead, we were no news. "J.R." was no news. Stringtown in Anderson County was no news. Hundreds of people behaving themselves were no news. It's one thing to breathe a sigh of relief and rejoice that "no news is good news." It's another thing to leave good news generally unreported as if it doesn't count for anything.

*David*

# THE KENTUCKY TRACE

$\mathcal{M}$aybe there should be a Kentucky Trace same as there's a Natchez Trace. On a trip to Mississippi in the summer of 1989, we decided we'd had enough of interstate highways and monstrosities such as the outer loop of Memphis, which should be arrested for impersonating civilization. We spent a night in a motel on the edge of Bowling Green, kept an appointment the next morning in Nashville, and then crossed over the Duck River on our way to Columbia, Tennessee, hometown of James K. Polk. He defeated Kentuckian Henry Clay for president in 1844, the third time Clay had been defeated for the presidency.

Hardly anybody 145 years later would know very much in a personal way about President Polk unless they took a detour from the interstate highway and drove toward a fine town such as Columbia, Tennessee. Others wouldn't know about Henry Clay if his home hadn't been preserved in Lexington, Kentucky.

The same is true of the Natchez Trace. Pick it up just outside of Columbia and for the next four hundred miles or so, be treated to one of those unique trips through history. Since the speed limit is fifty miles per hour and no commercial traffic is permitted (no billboards, no gas stations on the Trace itself, no fast food franchises), settle back and let your imagination take over.

"I never met a Kentuckian who did not have a rifle, a pack of cards, and a bottle of whiskey," said General Jackson at the Battle of New Orleans (thus sowing early stereotypical seeds). "Old Hickory" knew the Natchez Trace well, and he had some acquaintance with those "Kaintucks" who used the old trail on their overland return home after their flatboat trips down the Ohio and the Mississippi.

The Natchez Trace is soaked in blood–from before the time of Christ until the nineteenth century. Ancient Indian mound builders' work is still visible from the twentieth-century roadway. The Creeks, Cherokees, Choctaws, and Chickasaws suffered their own trail of tears. Even the great hunter and explorer Meriwether Lewis, who was named governor of Louisiana Territory in 1808 and was on his way to Washington, was either murdered or committed suicide on the Natchez Trace, October 11, 1809.

Now a smooth two-lane road meanders past Grinder's Stand, Buzzard Roost, Pontotoc, the Ackia Battleground, French Camp, Pigeon Roost, Doak's Stand, LeFleur's Bluff (which has become Jackson, the capital city of Mississippi), Grindstone Ford on Bayou Pierre, and Port Gibson, and finally arrives at Natchez.

Jonathan Daniels, who wrote "The Devil's Backbone" (apt name for the Natchez Trace), describes the old trail: "Down the Mississippi River they sold their cumbersome boats as lumber. And on the overland return by the Natchez Trace they sometimes brought back more gold clinking in their saddlebags than DeSoto's Spaniards vainly sought."

Sometime in the new century we ought to build a Kentucky Trace. We could start it out up near Covington. Then it might come down through Big Bone Lick State Park in Boone County, past Kincaid Lake in Pendleton County, through Blue Licks Battlefield State Park in Nicholas. We could bring it past Plum in Bourbon (where we promise not to open a watermelon stand), through the Boonesborough area in Clark and Madison, through the Central Kentucky Wildlife Management area. It would trickle on to Drip Rock down on the northern rim of Jackson County, to Mummie and Egypt on the eastern side of Jackson, through the Levi Jackson Wilderness Road State Park in Laurel County. It might pass Bailey's Switch in Knox County and the Dr. Thomas Walker State Shrine, and finally arrive at Jellico.

Speed limit: fifty miles an hour. Take time to smell the flowers. Instead of seeing how fast the trip can be made, ease up and see how long it takes. There's so much to see in home sweet Kentucky it's a puzzlement why anybody would want to spend money or time anyplace else. Some feel driven to travel anywhere and everywhere but Kentucky. With what the entire Commonwealth has to offer it makes sense to pick up a road map and take some detours.

*David*

# A Trip Back in Time

"*P*romise me one thing. If there's trouble in London or anywhere else in England, you won't call me to go and cover it," I said to Marcy McGinnis, CBS News vice president for Europe. We sat in her London Bureau Chief's offices overlooking Knightsbridge Road on one side, Hyde Park on the other.

She smiled in the direction of Lalie and me and devilishly made no such promise. She knew very well I would not be needed even if all other correspondents were elsewhere when the Thames reversed direction or mad cows stampeded Buckingham Palace.

Marcy said to give her a call if we needed help. I could tell there was a soft spot deep down in her news executive heart for a senior citizen from Plum Lick, Kentucky, who used to work for CBS News. He was the once-younger-and-thinner correspondent who covered Prince Charles's and Lady Di's wedding fifteen turbulent years before, the same year riots broke out in Liverpool and Belfast. From the vantagepoint of 1999, I think if I'd been in England or France at the time of Di's fatal wreck, I would have cowered someplace.

Fast rewind to the summer of 1996. Mission: a University of Kentucky research grant to study cholera epidemics of the nineteenth century with lessons to be learned for the twentieth and twenty-first. Our interest goes beyond cholera. If London, England, is the city of tomorrow, then what, pray tell, is the future of Kentucky? We ask ourselves this question as we ride on the Underground from Earl's Court Station, through Kensington, Belgravia, St. James's Park, and Westminster, to Embankment, where we transfer onward in the "Tube" to Tottenham Court Road.

"Mind...the...gap," is the stern, ominous, deep-throated warning to all as we step across the awkward space to the platform from this highly efficient, clean, politely ugly rapid transit system. It moves hundreds of thousands of faceless human beings, speaking many tongues, back and forth beneath the city, beneath the lives of poets, beneath monuments of conquering and vanquished heroes.

Nothing grows in the Underground. Hardly anything green grows above it except in parks, in scattered, manicured gardens, and in isolated flowerpots outside windows of end-on-end places of human habitation. Kentucky should not become this, we think, perhaps selfishly.

The British Museum, filled with priceless volumes–the original Magna Carta and manuscripts in the personal handwriting of Milton, Keats, Wordsworth, Browning, and Donne–is where we do the cholera research. We call up books in the historic Round Reading Room. From time to time we rest our eyes and our thoughts. We wander about the museum.

There's the incredibly preserved 2,000-year-old Lindow Man. There are the rooms full of timepieces stroking the passing of the moments. There are the groups of children from many nations making their pilgrimages for glimpses back in time to civilizations that have risen and fallen.

Here's the rub: how to ensure the green of the Plum Licks of the world, the home sweet Kentucky, while preserving an increasingly urban, intensely international metropolitan culture.

We walk down to Battersea Bridge to meet friends from Kentucky, England, and Scotland. On a Saturday evening we accompany them to St. Paul's Church in Knightsbridge. We're there to hear St. Paul's Festival Choir and Orchestra perform Verdi's Requiem. It is powerful and magnificent. Program notes sum up our yearning:

"Living at the pace most of us do, we need places like this, places which can be the 'still point' of the turning world."

On Sunday, we seek another "still point" outside the place called London. We board the train at Charing Cross and head east through Dunton Green, Sevenoaks, Paddock Wood, and Staplehurst. Here is the green. Here are the sheep. Here are the hedgerows. Here are the country roads. Here is reprieve.

We arrive at Dover and see the cliffs. We see the castle overlooking the English Channel. We walk past a church built in 1100. We stop for an hour at the Churchill Hotel on the waterfront. We read the World War I and II memorials, remembering the Kentuckians who died to keep England and America free.

Returning to London, we think we see more clearly the need to preserve the countryside and the city. One without the other will hasten the addition of one more fallen civilization to a museum of the future.

The express train departs London's King's Cross Station at mid-afternoon, slicing northward like a surgeon's knife at a top speed of 140 miles an hour with only two quick stops, in York and Newcastle. It's better than flying. The countryside is a swirl of agrarian images, like an overturned mail truck, its cargo of picture postcards caught in a sudden shift of wind. We're caught in a fantasy that more of Kentucky might look the same.

On to Morpeth, Pegswood, and Chathill, to Berwick on the coast of the North Sea, and in only a few more minutes the conductor will be making the announcement: "We're now crossing the border."

I've waited a lifetime of sixty-six years to visit Scotland. Something there is that has pulled me to it. It's worth the wait.

The land from North Berwick, Longniddry, and Wallyuford to Edinburgh is a place reminiscent of an older Kentucky. There are stone walls, stone bridges, stone houses, paddocks filled with sheep and cattle, tall hedgerows, lush fields of hay and winding streams, yet only a foretaste of sights to come a few days later on another train ride from Edinburgh to Inverness.

The upward climb from Perth through Blair Atholl includes stops at Dalwhinnie, Kingussie, and Aviemore. They illustrate what generations of committed, hard-working people can do with a land so craggy and stubborn that sometimes weeds, much less trees, refuse to grow. The Highlands reach the clouds as if shaking their fists like defiant fishmongers' wives. Young girls jig the dances at the annual Highland Games in Inverness, and let no Highland boy discount the strength in those turning legs, those tossing, outstretched arms with hands tightly fisted. And so, me lads, you've the tug of war to prove your manliness. You've the wire hammer, the shot, and the Scots hammer, and the fifty-six-pound weight to be heaving for height, and you've the tossing of the caber, if'n ye think ye're mon 'nough f'it!

For the lads and the lassies, there're the high jump and the relays and the running and the bicycle racing. Up in the stands and down-sprawled upon the cleanest of grass there are the spectators, the men and the women and the children, who know good things when they see them. There's no raucous behavior, no international soccer match violence, not even bad manners. It's the Olympics without all the folderol, all the corporate banditry.

The bagpipers play and the air is cool from the River Ness with never a need for a monster. And the children skip rocks and the waters sparkle with hardly a thing to mar them. "And do you notice how clean everything is?" says I to Lalie.

"Watch that man in the blue shirt," says she. "He's upended the caber twice now."

For Kentuckians who may be unfamiliar with it, tossing the caber would be a little like standing a young telephone pole on its end, lifting it up from the bottom, running with it, and flipping it so that when it lands it falls forward, not backward.

For home sweet Kentuckians looking for examples that encourage basic civility, it is possible to live without litter. It is possible to be stoic and simultaneously smiling and friendly. It is possible to take even the most forlorn of land and circumstance and do something with them as once described by Malachi Malagrowther (Sir Walter Scott: "The industrious and enterprising agriculturist or manufacturer...has converted Scotland from a poor, miserable, and barren country into one where, if nature has done less, arts and industry have done more."

"And will ye be a goin' to Skye?" asks the young waitress at breakfast the following morning.

"The Isle of Skye, you mean?"

"Aye, 'tis beautiful. I'll be goin' thar tamarra," she replies with the shyest of a Scot maiden's smile.

Well now. There's no reason to be waiting another sixty-six years, isn't that a fact now? For there're also the Isle of Mull, Rhum, Colonsay, Canna, Coll, and Tiree, and there're Lockmaddy on North Uist, Lockboisdale on South Uist, and Castlebay on Barra. Meantime, there're Robert Burns, Sir Walter Scott, and Robert Lewis Stevenson to be reading. There're our spiritual roots to be checking. There's home sweet Kentucky to be living. And even if we've not an ounce of Scotch-Irish blood in our veins, we'll claim it all the same.

*David*

# BOOTSIE

$\mathcal{I}$n search of an authentic individual, I found him just the other side of Cayce in Fulton County, almost as far west as you can go in Kentucky and still be in Kentucky. Hickman is a few miles farther across Highway 94, and still farther there's Ridge, Elbow Slough, and Willow Pond. Then there's that final westernmost little loop of the Commonwealth's toe that looks like an afterthought, a piece of Mississippi River capriciousness–the Beaver Slough neighborhood, hanging on to western sunsets like a lonesome skin tag.

The individual's name is Richard Nelson Henson. His father's name is Rollie Nelson Henson. His grandfather's name was Rollie Newton "Bootsie" Henson. Richard has a five-year-old son, Richard Nathan Henson. It's important to know all this because it explains the consistency of family connections in the initials "RNH" appearing on every broom Richard Nelson Henson makes with his hands, accompanied by a very determined look on his face. Richard Henson is more than a forty-seven-year-old maker of brooms.

"I'm proud to be a broom maker, but I'm much deeper than that," says Richard. We sit and talk amicably in his shop, converted in 1988 from a horse and goat barn to an internationally known and respected site on the edge of Mud Creek. Richard, maker of fine brooms with places to hang their handles in all fifty states and eight foreign countries, does not believe in mediocrity.

The handle of the broom is often made from a personally selected Kentucky pink dogwood tree, and the sweeping part is usually made from handpicked Mexican broomcorn (at one time a viable crop in the United States). Sometimes Richard and Nathan go out in the field and together they look for sedge to cut.

"When I make a broom, I mean for it to last. Of course, all brooms have a life too. But it'll be much shorter if you stand it on its head," the most important working part other than the handle. "When my brooms have finished [their lives] I want my customers to come back to me for more."

After twenty years of high school teaching, coaching, and school administrating, Richard Henson decided he wasn't happy with that kind of life. He'd had enough of the pressures, all the demands and expectations coming from so many different directions. The last thing Richard remembers his beloved grandfather, Bootsie, telling him, with a point of his finger, the night before he died: "As long as you're making brooms, you'll always have a job."

Being a strong, determined, independent, ego-driven individual is a "two-edged sword," Richard explained in late 1996. It has "allowed me to be creative, to perform on stage, entertain, allowed me to blossom," he confidently went on. "It's a balancing act with strength and weakness, and ego can get you in trouble," he said with a canny smile.

Richard Henson has traveled the Commonwealth and the adjoining regions (he won first place at the Malcolm Blue Storytelling Festival in Aberdeen, North Carolina, in late 1996), holding his audiences spellbound with a broom-making monologue reminiscent of Andy Griffith, Cotton Ivy, and the late Jerry Clower. But Richard doesn't copy them or anybody. He's his true self, a true grandson of Bootsie.

The television series Dr. Quinn has taken a liking to Richard Henson's brooms. His latest count is about eighty-eight that he has made especially for the show. When the characters sweep on that dusty program, they've usually done it with an RNH creation from the edge of Mud Creek in Fulton County.

*David*

# HORSE CAVE

$\mathscr{T}$o paraphrase Kentucky historian C.M. Dupier Jr., "If you would know the soul of Kentucky," take almost any exit from the interstate highway system.

Recently when crossing back into Kentucky, northbound on Interstate 65, we had an impulse to stop at the Welcome Center just south of Exit 2. (On the superroads in the Commonwealth exit numbers correspond to mile numbers.) It was on a winter morning, and we pulled in to ask about caves and "hidden" rivers. The lady on duty was friendly and helpful.

With maps and brochures to help us, we left the interstate at Exit 58 and drove two miles east on KY 218 into the community of Horse Cave (population 2,284 in the 1990 census). There was a parking place with our name on it, as they say, at the front door of the American Cave Museum.

Anybody who's visited the museum and the nearby Hidden River Cave knows what an exciting and educational opportunity is available to most. The descent into the cave has about 175 steep steps, so it's not for every visitor. One of the brochures calls it "a step into an unknown terrain where nature sculpts enormous subterranean chambers out of limestone."

Michelle Karle, the young caver on duty, explains the difference between the words "caver" and "spelunker." "Cavers usually rescue spelunkers," she says with a sympathetic smile.

After we've strolled through the two levels of museum exhibits we're ready to become "cavers." I remind myself that I don't have any business ever being a "spelunker."

We follow Michelle down the 175 steps, and it's like-well, it's like nothing seen out on any interstate highway. The air is eerily cool. Hidden River is flowing mysteriously with a consciousness of its own. The blind crayfish living on the sandbars stir with the presence of Michelle's flashlight as if signaling that they much appreciate total darkness.

There are the broken and abandoned turbine blades that once furnished lights to the Horse Cave community. There are the rusting pipes that once brought drinking water to the surface. In time, pollution spoiled both light and water possibilities. Now the American Cave Conservation Association is preserving nature's wonderment.

As you might imagine, going back up 175 steps is quite a bit different from going down them. But an old reporter and his wife pace themselves and are none the worse for wear.

It's time for lunch.

Now, we've done our share of franchise food hopping at many exits of the interstates and parkways. They're like chancy, rocky archipelagoes along the way to home cooking port. God is good to us when he causes us to find The Bookstore Cafè at 111 Water Street in Horse Cave, Kentucky.

Tom Chaney, one of the owners, greets us at the door. He's standing with a smile in the bookstore side. One step to the left is the Cafè side. In the middle are fried chicken, country ham, mashed potatoes, corn pudding, more vegetables, cornbread, biscuits, and about three kinds of desserts and cobblers.

We feast. Mercy.

And the price is right (better than two places we walked out of earlier when we floundered badly in the archipelagoes of northern Alabama).

We tell Tom how much we appreciate the food and the reasonable price. He says it's a mistake to charge too much and a mistake not to charge enough.

Not every enchanted island like the Bookstore Cafè leads to Walpole's serendipity, but there she is seated at the next table, Joy Bale Boone, one of Kentucky's poets laureate. She's with her husband, George Street Boone, Elkton attorney–two people who passionately care about the Commonwealth of Kentucky.

We begin to discuss one of my former professors of creative writing, the late Kentucky short story writer, novelist, and poet Hollis Summers. Tom Chaney appears from the bookstore side with a first edition of Summers's *The Weather of February*. And the price is right.

We've cheered and supported the interstate and parkway systems. But every once in a while it's wonderful to take one of the exits and go exploring for caves, poets laureate, books by former professors, hidden rivers, and the soul of Kentucky.

*David*

# GLASGOW

*O*ne of the important things that makes a community stand out is the people working together to achieve an uncommon goal. The cutting edge of success is having enough civic-minded people who don't care who gets the credit.

Glasgow, Kentucky, comes to mind. There are many municipal leaders who understand the wisdom of recognizing a need, stepping to the table where the talk is talked, then doing what it takes to produce results, letting the outcome speak for itself.

One of the centerpieces in Glasgow is the South Central Kentucky Cultural Center, where I was recently invited to speak. A converted tobacco warehouse, this facility celebrates the past and brings it alive with relics dating to the Revolutionary era. The collection bridges the nineteenth century and moves toward the twenty-first with new genealogical writings and histories by local authors. The Center is looking to move into a larger, renovated building that used to house a pants factory.

W. Samuel Terry IV, director of the Center, has prominently displayed a very fine French piano, a Pleyel, with a "perils of Pauline" history. It was produced in France, used in an opera house in Louisville, and raffled off as a prize, later emerged in the governor's mansion in Frankfort, was relegated to storage, finally donated to the South Central Kentucky Cultural Center, and at last restored by the Glasgow Music Club, oldest in the state.

Revolutionary war weapons and artifacts are some of the outstanding holdings at the Cultural Center. It includes the famous Settles Rifle made in Barren County and named for the renowned local gunsmith W.F. Settle. Nineteenth-century tools, clothing, and furniture are on display. There's the exceptional collection of work by the late Barren County historian Vivian Rousseau, including genealogical information on 350 families.

The former First Lady of Kentucky, Beulah Nunn, played a prominent role in the growth of the South Central Cultural Center.

As for the town, it's anything but a museum. South Green Street's vintage homes, many with lighted dogwood trees in the yards, are examples of the city's tradition of maintaining and preserving older residences. It's not every town in America under 13,000 population that has so many cultural opportunities. Sam Terry cites the music club, photography club, historical society, garden club and many civic organizations, all "doing things to better the community."

Glasgow is the home of Kentucky poet laureate Joy Bale Boone. It's also the hometown of many journalists: Diane Sawyer of ABC News; Julian Goodman, former president of NBC News; Bill Goodman, a current regular host on the Kentucky Educational Television Network; and Arthur Krock, formerly a reporter for *The Courier-Journal* and later Washington Bureau Chief for the *New York Times*. Politicians have been known to flower here. Former Governor Louie Nunn is a native of Glasgow, and it's the home of former Interim State Supreme Court Justice Walter Baker.

Glasgow is the location of one of five regional post-secondary education centers and there's a new elementary school as well as two industrial parks. The proximity of Barren River State Resort Park and Mammoth Cave has been a major factor in the growth of tourism.

Across from the Barren County courthouse there's a newly decorated monument to the homegrown composer, arranger and musician Billy Vaughn. It was he who wrote The Hilltoppers' big hit "Trying." The title fits the tempo of Glasgow today, which could be a model for other communities.

*David*

# KENTUCKY MUSIC

"*I*f music be the food of love, play on." Now there's a Shakespearean idea both lovely and powerful. It's well-suited to a Commonwealth that has produced music makers ranging in style from popular vocalist Rosemary Clooney to jazz vibraphonist Lionel Hampton; from country stars Loretta Lynn and Grandpa Jones to folksinger and composer John Jacob Niles, to balladeer Jean Ritchie, to Hugh Whitfield Martin, who sang at New York's Metropolitan Opera.

So we're not all country, not all jazz, not all classical–we're a blended essence of Shakespeare's "food of love," and it seemed there was no better time than Kentucky's bicentennial year, 1992, to establish the Museum of Kentucky Music and Hall of Fame. Some things take a little longer. By 1999, ground was still not broken, but the completion of the project was expected to be some time in 2001.

It has been a so-far-unfulfilled idea promoted by the museum's board of directors, growing and maturing out of a proposal approved in 1987 by unanimous vote in the Kentucky General Assembly. To be located at Renfro Valley, the nonprofit Museum of Kentucky Music and Hall of Fame will identify and commemorate for the first time in one place "a complete listing of all Kentucky musicians, vocalists, composers, and collectors."

Support for the facility has been as broadly based as the music itself.

Ronald Pen, professor of music at the University of Kentucky, says, "Jean Ritchie and John Jacob Niles have made the name Kentucky synonymous with vivid indigenous music...The museum would provide a most visible showcase for Kentucky's noted musical heritage."

Ron Sheets, president of the Kentucky Association of Electric Cooperatives, says, "All of our twenty-nine co-ops lend their strong philosophical support to the development of the museum."

Historian laureate Thomas D. Clark has written, "It would be a correct recognition of the fact that country music has ever been one of the Commonwealth's most substantial folk traditions and heritages."

John Conlee, a member of the board of directors, boldly proclaims, "Kentucky can be proud of the fact that there are no greater artists, and there are no more numbers of artists who had such an influence on music, as those who came from Kentucky." (Laying it on thick could be a forgivable stand to take in a state so long battered by stereotyping.)

As work on the facility proceeds, one of the most important jobs will be for each of the Commonwealth's 120 counties to search its collective memory for nominations. State legislators have been asked to name coordinators in each county. They will become members of the Friends of the Museum of Kentucky Music. Nominees for the museum will then become eligible for induction into the new music Hall of Fame.

It's important that the original idea of having only a country music hall of fame has been broadened to include jazz, blues, and pop artists, classical musicians, and others who don't fit within usual classifications. Renfro Valley appears ideally suited as a location because land there is available. While it's understandable that other communities would want to have this tourist attraction, Renfro Valley may best represent what George Zack, conductor of the Lexington Philharmonic believes when he says, "Such a facility will have an enormous capacity to produce economic, cultural, and artistic riches."

John Lair, founder of Renfro Valley, would most likely be proud that "country" has reached out to embrace other musical forms. Asher and Little Jimmy Sizemore, Aunt Molly Jackson, Merle Travis, Lonzo and Oscar, Dwight Yoakam, and many other "down home" music makers will make welcome Lee Luvisi, Robert Todd Duncan, and Edwin Franko Goldman, representing big-city classical musicians. It is hoped that they will feel comfortable in the company of their "country cousins."

"United We Stand, Divided We Fall" is a motto that can serve us all well in the preservation and celebration of Kentucky's rich tradition of music.

Byron Crawford of *The Courier-Journal*, has said it well: "Much of the museum's attention would focus on the evolution of Appalachian music from its early Scottish, Irish, and English ancestry to its twentieth century discovery by music scholars who are fascinated by its purity and rich tradition."

We'll be hearing a lot more about the Museum of Kentucky Music and Hall of Fame in coming days. Kentuckians from towns and counties throughout the Commonwealth may want to give a listen.

*David*

# Ninety-Seven Trombones

They played with their hearts and the tips of their upturned toes.

They played during the hot days of summer and the numbing, wet cold of late October.

The 1997 Kentucky Music Educators Association's Marching Band Championships rang clear and true throughout the Commonwealth. Then, on October 25, it came down to the finals in Commonwealth Stadium in Lexington.

These were not professional performers. They were not college students.

These were the best of the Commonwealth's high school students along with emerging talent from the middle schools.

In other words, they were kids!

They didn't look like kids. They demonstrated a level of maturity that might make a dent in the perception that typical secondary students today range from apathetic to zygodactyls (birds with two toes pointed forward and two backward).

The event was as stirring as any college football game, including the University of Kentucky overtime win over Alabama. Well, the goalposts didn't come down, but that wasn't necessary. The announcement of the champion bands in their various divisions was excitement enough for the students and their watchful, expectant parents.

How do you account for such dedication with recognition so relatively obscure? Some things resist explanation and may be impossible to pin down as well as a kid placing a talented finger on the hole of a flute.

It's a feeling as much as it is musicology. As with truth, it's like trying to nail jelly to a tree. But it's real, and you recognize it when you hear it and see it.

It begins in summer band camp. It starts with the directors saying,

"We're really serious about this, so listen up!"

Out in the parking lot, also known as a parade ground, the patterns of movement unfold through a series of stumbling and bumping into one another. Some notes are sour. Some are flat. Some are downright awful. There are tears. There are snappish exchanges when the trumpet player accidentally intrudes upon the territory of the trombone performer.

Soon something begins to click; yet sought-for magic doesn't happen like the genie popping from a bottle, saying, "You want to be the best marching band in your division in the Commonwealth?"

"Sure. That's what we want."

"O.K., it's yours!"

No, it doesn't work that way. Genies in bottles are better left for telling jokes.

Day after day, night after night, marathon session after marathon session come and go like reality checks as regular as metronomes with the exactness of chronometers.

The right tone evolves through a process of relentless practice. It's the sound that causes a judge to give the mark of excellence.

There's more than the sound of precision. There are the flags. They come in many sizes and colors. They must be positioned perfectly for the complex unfurling.

The timing of the display of the flags, woven into the fabric of the music and the formations of the feet, creates an excitement through extraordinary visual surprises. For the first time in their lives, kids are known as flags. There's something nice about that, something exhilarating in the escape from hellish, hormonal frustrations to emerge into a beautiful, fluid world of sight and sound.

None of this works without the pit crew. Mainly, these are the dads who break the stereotypes of the Great Hunters stalking their prey. Moms are also down in the pit, and there are students of all ages who, for whatever reason, are not out on the field of dreams. They're all working the sidelines with split-second timing as efficiently as the pit crews at the Indianapolis 500.

There are the drum majors or field commanders who signal the start and the finish of the performance with their salute and traditional, raised, clinched fist. It's a gripping moment for band directors, parents, pit crewmembers, and friends. There's no more time for mentoring.

The kids are on their own. They're flying. They're soaring. They know what it's like to win and to lose.

Marching bands represent 160 schools on the district level. They become 122 at the regionals. Only sixty-five–4,486 playing members, 1,251 auxiliary members (flags), and 92 drum major or field commanders–make it to the semifinals. They become the sweet sixteen at four levels in the championships at Commonwealth Stadium.

From the biggest, like Lafayette, to the smallest like Nicholas County, there are the tall, shining trophies to place on the shelves of honor at the respective schools.

For everyone who competes there will be the perpetual place in the hearts of those who've come to understand the importance of KMEA's Kentucky Marching Band Championships.

For those who came close this year but didn't win first place, ahead are new opportunities, beginning with band camp next summer!

*David*

# PART TWO

*The college professor, who was headed for his shepherd's clothes, stopped and listened.*

*"Maa. Maa. Maa," returned the sound.*

# LITTLE LAMB

*T*he trouble with being a shepherd is the pain that goes with the loss of a lamb. No matter how many times death is encountered, the feeling is the same–a deep sense of helplessness.

The burial of the orphan lamb did not symbolize for all time for all lambs as if it were the tomb of an unknown soldier.

"Damn," muttered the shepherd as he came upon another lifeless form stretched upon the straw bedding of the lambing barn. The form was long and slender, like a white glove crinkled and tossed upon a pallet.

He picked it up and carried it outside to the old truck bed, leaving the tiny body there as if to compromise between an open ditch and a forsaken spot on the other side of the fence by the machine shed.

"I'll do something about it later," were words spoken deep in thought as the Dorset and Suffolk rams watched to see if some ground corn might be added to their feeding pail.

As the shepherd walked back from the barn, his footsteps made a muffled sound in the ooze of January thaw. The outline of the barn blended into the steel gray of the star-speckled sky. Lady, the guard dog, stretched in the ram lot but made no sound, only the sighs that came from yawning deeply. The Dorset and the Suffolk lowered their heads at the dimming prospect of a midnight snack of ground corn.

"Lambs are going to die, that's a fact, but I sure wish they wouldn't," were words spoken against the night.

"You want them to live so they can die when you want them to," said Orion, the Great Hunter, swaggering sideways over Bunker Hill. The shepherd looked up at his old friend, who had traveled with him throughout the world. There was a groan of resignation.

The evening drive home from the university had become less joyful of late. Even the night of the triplets and the four sets of twins, plus a strong and sturdy single lamb, did not quite dispel the gloom, for two more bodies were slung upon the old truck bed.

Fatigue was setting in.

"Should not have built the pens this way. Too much chance for separation.

Next year, it'll be different. Each ewe will have a pen at least one week before she's due. The bottom panels will be high enough to prevent one lamb wandering off before the next one is born. That's what happened to two sets of twins, and all four lambs died. It was my fault, all my fault."

It was late one night while walking up to the old house that faces west, just above the spot where a hundred years ago there had been a training track for horses. There was a sound as tiny as a bell tinkling, borne on the night air from the area of the water well past the maples to the side porch.

The college professor, who was headed for his shepherd's clothes, stopped and listened.

"Maa. Maa. Maa," returned the sound.

He backed up the car and pointed the headlights in the direction of the water well. Nothing. He left the car running and walked across the bottom where, in another century, five-gaited horses had racked in their glory. Nothing. But as he came closer to the exact spot, there was the lamb, lost from the rest of the flock.

Crooked in the arm and carried back to the barn, the lamb was snug and silent. Something had bitten its tail in half. The drops of blood were bright red. Perhaps Lady, the guard dog, had done it in a desperate effort to move all the flock before night fell. The lamb, placed in a bedding of straw, waited

while a bottle of milk warmed at the house. None of the ewes was interested in the lamb. It nursed some from the nipple but not much.

After two days, the lamb with half of a tail disappeared. After that there was a shift in the stars.

Night after night, more lambs were born. They lived. One ewe birthed a remarkable set of twins. They were as strong as some earlier lambs had been weak. They were quickly on their feet for the first nursing, going after their mother's milk like nose tackles going after Joe Montana.

"Death in the lambing barn is more than compensated by the living," the shepherd thought. On a clear night, the Big Dipper was inverted between the eaves of the barn and the sycamore tree, while the Great Hunter was sliding down the sky.

*David*

# Spinning Thoughts

$\mathcal{W}$hile waiting for the delivery of our new spinning wheel, we've been spending extra time in the lambing barn. It's out of control.

We can't seem to do anything right. About as many lambs are dying as are being born. It's awful. It began with the big and beautiful lamb that didn't survive even a few minutes because the covering membrane wasn't removed from its face. Like an idiot, I watched the birth and thought everything was fine. But by the time I returned after going to the house to tell everybody the good news, the lamb was dead. The ewe had not done what nature said she should have–removed the membrane. She had a vacant stare.

Lambs caught in narrow slats, lambs born outside in the middle of the night, lambs lain on by their mothers, lambs disowned and butted out by their mothers–with a hundred ewes birthing at all hours of the day and night it's enough to make you wish the damned spinning wheel would come so something could be done that's predictable and controllable.

Being a part-time shepherd is not what the Shepherd of us all had in mind. "Being There" is what it's all about. You just can't go off and leave your flock to its devices. If you do, you're asking for trouble. Sometimes even being there is not enough, but it's a step in the right direction.

I bristle when people say, "Sheep are stupid," but sometimes I have to own up to it: faced with the simplest of decisions, a sheep will more times than not do the wrong thing. It's also a fact that they seem to have a fascination, even a yearning, about dying. They lie down and slip into the big sleep as if it were a warm glove on a cold night. Let them get sick and you might as well forget it. "Sheep make poor patients," according to one local veterinarian.

What all this means is that we are in the middle of the lambing season, and we're running low on energy and patience. We've only got so much of each. When the shepherd starts yelling at her/his sheep and rapping them on the nose with ears of corn, you know it's time to sit down at the spinning wheel and calm down.

When I ran into Charles Kuralt one day in Lexington, he asked how my retirement was going. "Down the slippery slope with the sheep," should have been my reply. But I took a positive view, as you'd expect most shepherds to do. Shepherding is a good sounding word, and people tend to return a warm smile when told that's what you believe yourself to be (sheep or no sheep). What other mortals don't know is the price paid for this station in life. "The good shepherd giveth his life for the sheep," according to St. John, but the peak of the lambing season is enough to drive the holiest of shepherds totally out of their gourds. Most of the ones I know are in favor of shepherds deciding when sheep are slaughtered, rather than the sheep signing the death warrants of the shepherds. That's why it'll be good for the new spinning wheel to arrive. It may be the therapy the shepherd needs before he goes off and does something he may regret.

*David*

# OLD DOGS AND LITTLE DIGITS

*W*e've all had those mornings when we've risen from sleep with the optimism of Norman Vincent Peale. We glide. We sally forth on the golden wings of angels.

"Visualize your fears as being drained out of your mind and the visualization will in due course be actualized," was an idea I'd begun to practice thirty years before as a result of rereading Dr. Peale's Power of Positive Thinking.

Early on a recent glory day I moved through the house as quietly as possible so as not to awaken those who value so highly the colorful dream possibilities of dawn's first light. I padded silently in my stocking feet, opening and closing doors without once clicking them, much less slamming them.

Silence had become my strategy and my virtue.

First I went to the kitchen to prepare my favorite breakfast (and the only one worth mentioning). That's two sausage patties, one egg sunny side up (I've never learned to flip them over with any predictability), two pieces of toast (one for the egg, one for blackberry jam), and coffee with a touch of milk.

The sausages browned ever so nicely and the egg did not stick to the skillet. The toaster performed admirably and the imitation butter spread evenly. I thought it only decent to invite in Dirk, the German shepherd, and I rewarded him with a pinch or two of the crust of the toast.

By the time of the second cup of coffee I was in what Dr. Peale would call "A Peaceful Mind Generating Power." I was ready for the world. I had neither harangued nor hectored anybody. I hoped to be remembered fondly for such generosity and sensitivity.

It was at this moment that I decided to treat Dirk to a can of premier dog food mixed with the usual dry stuff, which, presented by itself, he barely tolerates and avoids until there's nothing else standing between him and starvation.

I went to the pantry, taking a look down the hallway to be sure my peaceful mind had not generated so much power that it had awakened the sleeping angels.

I removed a roll of paper towels in order to find the can of dog food that Dirk loves almost as much as a freshly killed lamb. I took out the can, set it on the counter, and proceeded to push the roll of paper towels back into place.

It was at this point that Norman Vincent Peale's "Prescription for Heartache" descended upon me with the speed of a bolt of lightning. A heavy, glass bottle of syrup fell from the top shelf.

Warehouses of optimism did not repeal gravity. The bottle took the shortest route from the top shelf to my previously undefiled right big toe.

No words could describe the pain.

I leaned into the doorjamb, a gasp arising from the area of the arch of my foot. By the time it reached my vocal cords it had vanished in a sea of misery. I wondered if a cannibal had spent the night in the pantry and was bent on spearing a juicy breakfast. About this time another jar of syrup zapped the floor inches from the wounded big toe. Sensing a hunting party I retreated to a chair and mustered up the courage necessary to remove the sock and observe the damage.

It looked O.K., but something told me not to touch it. I put on my shoes and headed for the tobacco barn and spent the rest of the morning in the stripping room. This probably was not the best of ideas.

By midday my right big toe looked like a piece of anthracite, sometimes known as hard coal, the kind that burns real good with a "clean flame."

The doctor's assistant who looked at it said it was the ugliest big toe she'd ever seen. I was told that only time could cure such an injury. With this in mind I declined an x-ray and passed up pain pills.

That same night I spoke to Boy Scout officials in Mercer County. I told them that the Scout motto "Be Prepared" begins with putting your shoes on before looking after the other dogs.

Footnote/Toenote:

I am happy to report that the badly aggrieved phalange has regained its normal color and the nail, surprisingly, does not seem doomed. However, it's never too late for old dogs to learn new tricks. Sir Isaac Newton and I have come to terms with the advantages and challenges of gravity. Without it we'd be flying dogs and syrup bottles.

*David*

# THE VOICE

*I*'m finding it increasingly difficult to leave home sweet Kentucky for just about any reason. A trip in the first week of February to beautiful downtown Gainesville, Florida, was almost enough to sap the last ounce of energy from my body. Here it was the middle of winter on Plum Lick, while down there students were running hither and thither in shorts and sandals as if it were the merry, merry month of May.

Let's clear up this sort of nonsense. February is February and May is May, and nobody has any business messing with them. On the other hand, Kentucky is Kentucky and Florida is Florida–apples and oranges, so to speak. That being the case, I suppose I shouldn't have been surprised to find the Gainesville weather so unwinterly from a Plum Lick point of view.

Anybody who departs the invigorating invitations of winter in Kentucky for the balmy blandness of a Gainesville, Florida, in February, deserves what he or she gets: enough humidity to give off a royal headache; enough heat to stultify most imaginations; enough sweat to distort normal vision. It's strictly for the snowbirds and the regular natives.

The sad part of it is that they may never know the satisfying feeling of bringing an armload of homegrown, personally cut firewood to the hearth. What does a Gainesvillian know about the joy of laying and then lighting dry kindling? And what of the pleasure that comes from having a nice supply of country matches to strike as needed? Who would trade the crackling warmth of a bright new fire for the artificial wheeze of an air conditioner?

Well, I suppose I'm outnumbered, and that's all right. As long as about thirteen million people (not counting snowbirds) are basking in the sun in Florida, that means there're thirteen million people I don't have to deal with while building a nice little fire on Plum Lick.

I mean, just consider the role played in all this by the Atlanta airport, which was obviously designed to serve as Purgatory for wayward sinners. Stepping from the plane toward Concourse A, B, C, D, or T is not unlike what an innocent animal must feel after leaving the unloading chute. I'm not sure that humans were made for this sort of thing. Maybe that's why I felt so little like a human as I plunged ahead from Concourse A to get to Concourse D to make my connection. Have you noticed that the master plan seems to include arriving at A and departing from D, or arriving at D and departing from A? It causes a country boy to wonder if it ever occurred to any of the people-movers that it would make a whole bunch of sense to arrive and depart from A, or arrive and depart from D. That would be something like seeing how close you can hold a match to the kindling, not how far away you can hold it, and expect something worthwhile to happen.

As for the length and angle of the escalator that takes you from the concourse down to the train stations, all I can say is, Aunt Florence would have loathed and despised it. Before she died at the resolute age of ninety-five, having cut across the nineteenth and twentieth centuries, Aunt Florence avoided escalators as most of us do boa constrictors. The towering escalators in the Atlanta Airport would have given Aunt Florence a terminal case of vertigo. Whether going up them is worse than going down them is a matter of individual fear and loathing. I think dear Aunt Florence would have taken one look to the top and thrown such a fit the security folks would have had to bring out the net and haul this feisty little person off to the hoosegow.

The subway trains in the Atlanta airport are some slick devils too, all right, and you sure can't fault them for dragging their feet (even if they do drag yours loose from their ankle moorings). But it's THE VOICE that is the embodiment of all that is unearthly in the Atlanta airport. Some of us have grown reasonably accustomed to mechanical voices thanking us for direct dialing our telephone calls, but the voice of the conductor of the trains beneath the Atlanta airport takes unfriendliness to new frontiers. If you've heard it, you know what I'm talking about. If you haven't, I don't know if I can describe it. It's something like a very wicked person with a bad cold talking up a rusty downspout.

"Stop! This train is leaving." Or something like that.

My paranoia causes me to believe that if you disregarded the warning the closing doors would cut you in half and nobody would waste a second to pick up the pieces.

The subway trip from A to B to C and finally to D makes me feel like a bowling ball–hard, smooth, and very fast. Everything is color coordinated; otherwise a reasonably thoughtful person might be disoriented. Being lost in the Atlanta airport is a condition not to be visited on even the worst sinner among us.

Leaving the Atlanta airport is not unlike the joy one knows at graduation time. Even lingering in the long line of planes waiting to take off is a time for celebration. At least you're left with the impression that you really are about to go someplace.

I didn't go to Gainesville because I knew anybody there. That would have made too much sense. I went as a member of an accrediting team to visit the University of Florida. The main anomaly as far as I was concerned was the "beautiful" weather. As I looked at all those beautiful young people in their shorts, riding their fancy bicycles, I couldn't help but wonder if they weren't missing something important. They were missing the opportunity to carry in firewood, build the kindling just so, and watch the flames on a hearth reach for the top of the locust logs, spreading warmth and cheer on a three-dog night in home sweet Kentucky.

I decided not to talk to them about it.

*David*

# JUGGLING FLOCKS

$\mathcal{T}$he difficulty--almost the impossibility–of being a good part-time shepherd is weighing heavily on me. The Lord knows, I give it every ounce of strength in my body, but there's only so much that's handy.

Up at five o'clock (sometimes it's four-thirty), and it's all I can do to stumble to the bathtub to restart the circulation in my arms and legs. By then, I'm in no mood to put on foul weather gear, including boots about as comfortable as gloves with rocks in the fingertips.

I know if I go to the barn and discover a ewe having trouble birthing her lambs, there's no time to help. I have to be on my way to the university where teachers have to arrive early in order to discover something as miraculous as a parking place. So I head for the yellow brick road, Interstate 64. Along the way I listen to National Public Radio, which from time to time has wonderful little, precious stories about the glories of being a shepherd. I think they need a report from me about what it's like to be a part-time shepherd.

As director of the School of Journalism, I juggle students, faculty, budget, curriculum, committee meetings, speaking engagements, publishing house representatives, educators' associations, new laws, equipment failures, paper clip shortages, software updates, space allocations, spelling bees, the KBA (broadcasters), the KPA (newspapers), the SPJ (Society of Professional Journalists), the NABJ (black journalists), PRSSA (public relations), AAF (advertising), textbooks, supplies, copy machines, pencil sharpeners, fund-raising, letter writing, memo writing, alumni relations, complaints, and leaking urinals.

When I struggled up to the front porch of my "retirement" home in Camelot on a recent night, it occurred to me that I had put in another thirteen-hour day, which is about typical. I kissed and hugged my wife and child, put on my sheep's clothing, and headed down to the barn.

The sheep see me coming and they run to meet me. It's not because they love me but because I represent something to eat and they are hungry. I go to the corncrib and sit on the edge inside the door. One at a time I pitch ears of corn with both hands, and with my feet I fend off the more aggressive ewes. If I'm not careful they'll have me for supper.

Lordy, I'm tired. But they're hungry and I must feed my flock. I take a ration of corn and hay to my feeder lambs soon to be on their way to somebody's table, and I check to see if the ewe I've penned up has had her lambs. You'd think there'd be a little reward in all this for the good ole part-time shepherd, and sometimes there is. It's watching a dozen three-week old lambs playing "King on the Mountain." They run stiff-legged as hard as they can to the top of a manure pile, and they see who can stay on summit the longest. Then they come down and run in circles like colts in a paddock. They kick up their heels and pummel the ground by the soft light of the moon. I've considered joining them, but it would not make the best of pictures for paparazzi lurking behind the sycamore tree.

For a few precious moments there are no committee meetings, no budget cuts, nor any students with scheduling problems. There's the sheer joy coming at the end of a long day when the part-time shepherd returns home to tend his flock.

*David*

# TWIN BLESSINGS

$\mathcal{I}$t was about 1:45 in the morning. Before I could go to sleep, I wanted to write about something that had happened just after midnight at the lambing barn.

I had rousted myself from a warm bed, pulled on my foul weather gear, and gone out into the frightfully cold night, the tail of what the weather forecasters were calling the 1992 Alberta Clipper. The wind was so sharp it cut like a razor blade. I told myself I wouldn't have wanted to be stranded in it. A wind chill factor of twenty below zero can kill real fast.

I made it down the slope to the barn without slipping and falling. It wasn't snowing any more as we had expected earlier. But what had fallen had stuck, and it was slick. The water in the wet weather runoff by the side of the barn had almost iced over. It was a night not fit for man or beast.

The wind was blowing so hard the barn door was a lethal weapon. Prying it open took almost more strength than I had in my aching body. Getting in the way of it when it banged shut would be like getting hit by a Canadian cannonball.

When I finally opened the door, I looked down into pen number one. There they were! Our best homegrown Dorset ewe had just had twin lambs. I didn't have words to express the satisfaction I felt—even more so because the first-born had become stuck between two slats in the pen and probably would have died if I hadn't gotten myself out of bed and gone to check on the flock.

The next thing I did was to hold the lambs up to see whether they were boy lambs or girl lambs. Twin ram lambs is a very good happening when you're dealing with registered stock. It means there's a likelihood that twins are in the genes and the trait will be passed along. I picked up the larger of the two lambs: a ram. I picked up the second of the two lambs: another ram!

I went to the loft and brought down half a bale of clean straw and spread it evenly in the pen to give the ewe and her lambs a warmer and dryer place to spend the rest of the night. I put iodine on the lambs' navels and made sure the ewe's milk was flowing.

I was ready to dance a jig, even on such a cold night as this, the coldest night of the year so far–about zero. I checked on the rest of the flock and didn't find any more lambs. I didn't want to find any more. I had all the satisfaction I could handle. Well, almost.

I climbed back into the pen with the ewe and her ram lambs, and I lay in the clean straw and listened to the soft, mothering sounds as the Alberta Clipper whimpered and ran off to the northeast. It wouldn't have mattered if it were forty below zero. I had the warmth and the feeling of new life in abundance. Nothing else mattered. The ewe didn't seem to mind, so I stayed for a portion of the early morning hour.

When I climbed back out of the pen to return to the house and stepped outside, a piece of cold moon hung over Plum Lick. I looked up at it and wondered how my ancestors had tended their sheep and managed to stay warm here a hundred years ago. I imagined it hadn't changed too much.

I walked slowly back to the house. Before I went to bed I wrote down the joy I had just known. I whispered "I love you" to Lalie, turned off the light, and went to sleep.

*David*

# CHANGES

It has started again. We've been watching it for a couple of weeks. It's always such a pleasant sight.

The jonquils have pushed up in their wagon wheel design on the south side of the house. The pattern is a dark green. In recent days the flower part has been aching to burst, and although it seems too early for it, there's no denying the annual warming of the good earth.

Out in the bottom where the wheat was sown for a cover crop after last year's tobacco cutting, the green is growing almost before our eyes. The same thing is happening on the other side of the driveway where the lower-lying bottom has been sowed with a variety of grasses. Later this summer it'll look good square-baled and snug in the loft of the stock barn. Next winter it'll feel good to be pushing it down through the opening in the loft floor.

One of these times we're going to have a winter worthy of the name. I keep saying this, and all we have are these unnatural, not as beneficial, mild "winters" that are good only for the city folks. For farmers they mean less heaving and conditioning of the soil. They also mean a larger insect population. One of these times we're going to have ten-foot high snow banks like those we used to have about forty years ago.

The birds have been making their pre-spring ruckus in the water maples. These are the trashy birds, the disheveled and disorderly ones that precede the robins. Any day now we're expecting the arrival of the robin scouts, and soon after, the main force of cheeky redbreasts will appear on the scene. It takes time. Edwin Way Teale, who wrote the series of fine books on the seasons, said, in his *North with the Spring*, that the season of renewal moves northward at about fifteen miles a day. "Each season, like each human being and each puppy, is an individual, unique."

What Teale says is true and the approach of the spring of 1992 has caused me to be more optimistic, even in the face of a recession that knows no season. Perhaps that's the key to overcoming a dreadful economy and ills of every kind. Optimism, newfound hope, and leaps of faith will prevail.

The lambs are arriving regularly now, and more of them are surviving. The calves are dropping with ease and rising to nurse without difficulty. Pulling calves and bottle feeding them is not the way to go. We're beginning to look for that especially warm and dry day when we can put our plows down and turn the soil for this year's crop. The challenges of gardening–vegetables and flowers–are close at hand. They usually come the end of the first week in May, right after the Kentucky Derby, but now is the time to go to sleep reading seed catalogues.

We have two new purple plum trees to plant by the front entrance, and that will become a special weekend for the family. Planting trees is among the most underrated joys, unless it's the thrill of experiencing the blossoms. The days, the weeks, and the months of winter have sped by so fast we wonder where the time has gone. Only yesterday, it seems, there was the beginning of autumn. The magic of the seasons is one of the major reasons why we love Kentucky so much.

*David*

# CAPRICIOUSNESS

The first day of spring is a miracle unfolding. But it's not as simple as stepping from the cold of one season to the warmth of another. Technically, in the Northern Hemisphere spring stretches from the vernal equinox to the summer solstice. Technicalities are one thing, realities are another.

"Whatcheer...whatcheer...whatcheer" has been sounding outside our bedroom window, well before the sun has once again headed northward. The Kentucky Cardinal cardinalis's "whatcheer" had been our encouragement well before a radio announcer told us that spring had begun on March 21, 1992.

Then there were the robin scouts strutting across our front yard. They've returned! Soon the redbreast army will arrive and there'll be fierce competition for the worms and insects climbing up from their winter doldrums.

The lambs born since New Year's Day nod in the warmth of the sun by day, curl together beneath the corncrib in the cold of the night's full moon. On warm afternoons on the sides of the hills the new calves run and kick up their hind hooves; they hunker down in the woods when the wind, as if to keep the creatures honest, comes whipping up the valley.

Officially it's spring, but there's still a chance for snow as late as May. Spring is like that. It's as unpredictable as life itself. There are no guarantees, and we accept that as a part of what makes so special the season of birth. Some lambs and calves don't make it. Some die for no apparent reason. There are many imperfections, but success is achieved through the preponderance of numbers. Nature assures perpetuity of the species by overcompensation.

Sometimes a helping hand makes a difference. The lamb separated from its mother had taken refuge alongside the rear wheel of the big farm truck. One more night and the lamb would certainly have died. We brought the lost creature into the kitchen, fed it milk from a bottle, gave it a warm spot on the furnace grate, and went to bed with the hope that the lamb might live.

There was a bleat in the night. The mother of the house fed the lamb again, and it went back into a deep sleep. We thought there'd be a dead lamb in the morning, but when we woke up there still was life. We administered an antibiotic, and it seemed to make a difference. The lamb was returned to the flock, and it was Mother Nature's turn again.

A neighbor's cow was in trouble. It was a breach birth and time was running out. We walked the herd to the holding pens and sorted out the cow with the one small foot presented. We secured the distressed cow in the head gate, and removed the lifeless calf.

That's how spring really is. There is life and there is death, and it takes the latter to appreciate the former. There is warmth and there is cold, and it takes the negative to help us savor the positive. Spring is not always gentle, not always friendly. It's a capricious time of the year and should not be faulted for it. We're just thankful it's here again.

*David*

# DOGWOODS IN BLOOM,
# THREAD IN THE LOOM

*T*he blossoming boughs of April have outdone themselves this year. Down at Beaver Dam, across Rough River, and on to the Ohio River the dogwood is in spectacular blossom. Throughout the Commonwealth millions of dogwood are flowering, but especially in the area of Browns Valley and Dundee the scene is breathtaking.

Robert Browning's "All the breath and the bloom of the year in the bag of one bee" has tempted me to stop and take unto myself one blossom–just one–for dogwood bouquets are best suited, as are some rare humans, to live in nature rather than out of it. The captured loveliness must be studied quickly because, once removed from its fragile connection, the dogwood blossom fades very fast.

There are four bracts, thin and candy cream-colored with hints of purple at the slightly down-turned tips. They are anchored to a pliant, pale green stem at the base of which there are four miniature leaves. The woodier stem makes the crucial connection to the dogwood twig, which draws the juice of life up from the soil, a process that repeats itself each spring in all parts of home sweet Kentucky.

At the heart of the flowering process is a cluster of sixteen buds surrounding one in the center of the threshold, which is the leading edge about to burst forth. The blossom is in the precious moment of reproduction, leaving me to wonder if my curiosity is justified. I return home to Plum Lick, climb the old wooden steps to the study, and take down from the shelf William Carey Grimm's *The Book of Trees*, where it has been sleeping all winter.

"Man will live a fuller, happier life if he knows the trees that abound by his home." Words from the foreword of Grimm's definitive work are a reminder to stop and study as well as smell the flowers. The author's description of the habitat of the flowering dogwood is a reminder, too, that nature has its own plans for abandoned land. Fencerows become fertile places for untended beauty. The dogwood is contented and well suited for the role of "under-story" tree in forests of mightier creations.

But of what use is the little dogwood? Beyond its sudden burst of glory, what's to be said for it in an age of burgeoning development, technological sophistication? Nineteenth-century women boiled the dogwood root for a tea to combat fever, a substitute for quinine.

"John, I'll be needing some dogwood root."

"I'll bring it back at dinner time."

"No," said the young woman, Cynthia, who was my great-grandmother, "I'll be needing it before then. Bill's fever needs to be down."

"I'll go now."

Great-grandfather John went to the woods behind the old house in Joshua Meadows, and he dug from the ground the dogwood root Cynthia needed for Billy, my grandfather. The fever came down, and Billy lived. He became straight and tall, a suitable lad for Laura, who lived in another old house farther up Plum Lick Creek. They were married not knowing that their bliss derived from the sweetness of the dogwood.

Each year the dogwoods have produced their blossoms, and it has become old fashioned to boil the dogwood root to produce the tea to make the fever come down. Drugstores have replaced dogwoods.

I remember when I was a little boy, my mother, the daughter of Bill and Laura, used to say that, of all the seasons, autumn was the one she preferred, but of all the blossoms of spring, the dogwood was her special fancy.

*David*

# New Life

*I* have an annual annoyance with bunny rabbits, baby ducks, and Easter pets in general, but not even the sight of a chocolate cross in a display of religious candy could tempt me to play a springtime Scrooge.

I feel sorry about the fate soon to befall a raft of rabbits, a deck of ducks, and a plethora of pets. I can hardly describe my dismay upon seeing a child devouring a chocolate cross; however, I'm too excited about what I see all about me to worry too much about such strange human behavior.

There's fulfillment in the knowledge that Kentucky is as green as Ireland. Never mind the complaints that it's raining with some regularity (as if there was no causal relationship between rain and green grass). Never mind that shoes are known to become touched with mud while walking along the creek, and never mind that the sun is taking a rest from its intensive labors. The grass is gloriously green, and that's what warms my heart and possibly my soul.

The cattle and the sheep are in heaven. For days now they've eschewed the rolled hay we put out for them all winter; they're a-chewing the young, green shoots of pasture that are so delicious it'll make them sick if we don't put out medicated salt as a supplement. As my banker friend and distant cousin Harvey Crouch puts it: it's the time of year when calves and lambs jump with stiff-legged delight.

Have you also noticed that the thistles are here? I'm talking about the nodding thistles, the kind that grow as large as young trees. These aren't the smaller, pesky bull thistles but the aggressive and prolific nodding thistles, which if left unchallenged will turn a field into an impassable forest of willful weeds as high as a tall person's head. Nodding thistles have taproots that reach far down into the subsoil; chopping the growth off at the surface means only a challenge to this most stubborn and aggressive weed. Nodding thistles produce a purple flower that evolves into a silky mass. When the wind blows, the thistledown takes wing, flying from farm to farm, unmindful of such ridiculous notions as fences.

A good and energetic farmer, as was Hilton Windley, steward of this soil before we arrived to take our turn, might have his land completely clean of the damnable nodding thistle only to have it filled up again by the invasion of the innocent-looking thistledown from miles away. You see, all is not green grass even in the best of times. Some is nodding thistle.

So we take the bad with the good, as, I suppose, I should be accepting of bunny rabbits and chocolate crosses at Easter.

Wayne came over to the house after nightfall, and he asked if I'd like to go with him to see if one of our cows had given birth to her calf. Naturally I said I wanted to do that, because this would be my celebration of Easter. All I would need would be to see one small calf for one shining moment. We went in the four-wheel drive because the recent rains have made the hillsides muddy. When we crossed Plum Lick Creek the water slapped the floorboard and jostled the empty Ale-8 bottles. We drove over to the Old Jim Crouch Place, where the herd of cows and calves had settled in for another wet night. The mama cow that had been trying to have her calf was nowhere in sight. We crisscrossed the draws to the back of the big field, but still no cow in labor. We drove to the top of the hill from where we could see the lights of homes stretching from Plum to Bunker Hill.

As we came down the other side, there she was. Had she had her calf? Yes. It was lying in the tall grass left over from last year. It was warm and safe in the new grass coming on. The mama cow didn't want us there. The headlights of the four-wheel drive confused her. The new calf struggled to its feet. Bull calf. Its grandmother was Aberdeen Angus, its grandfather was Simmental, and its father was Brahma. The genetics put smiles on our faces. Big calf. Healthy. Doing all right. We wanted not.

The drive back to the house was pleasing. We stopped at the barn to look at the sheep. They were in out of the rain. We scratched the ram's head. He likes that. We rattled the feed bucket to make sure everybody was all right. They were.

And so were we.

*David*

# WAGGING THEIR TAILS

*T*he shepherd is standing by an open gate; his sleeves are rolled up, his hands are resting on his staff. The sheep dog is steadying the small flock of ewes and the ram, easing them through the gap. The hedgerow is dense, the fields lush. Trees are huge and gnarled. The sea completes the landscape off on the horizon.

It's England, Ireland, or Scotland as seen through a Charles J. Adams lithograph. The shepherd, his sheep, and his dog cause a Kentuckian, weary of another day of mankind and machines, to long for a few simple pastoral pleasures. Life is too fast too much of the time, anyway.

"You look tired," says a well-meaning colleague in the College of Communications.

"I am tired," is the reply.

Instead of counting sheep, the shepherd who missed his calling counts deadlines. Deadlines, decisions, and dilemmas are the orders of the day. "Deadlines amuse me," is the M.A.S.H. retort on the wall of the little weekly newspaper in that part of Kentucky that resembles the English, Irish, and Scottish countryside.

Anybody amused by deadlines is doubtless missing them. The reality is that deadlines must be met and there's no excuse for either ignoring or being amused by them.

"Where were you today?"

"Oh, I was out with the maa-maas." (Contrary to popular belief, sheep don't "baa"–they "maa." They're monolabial, meaning they've learned to make the "m" sound but not the "b" sound. Listen to them carefully sometime. The Tommy Thumb who wrote "baa-baa black sheep" didn't spend much time with the real thing.)

"How does it happen that you missed the meeting?"

"I was out looking for Ewedawg."

"You what?"

"Yeah. See, I had this dog named Ewedawg, and she was supposed to protect the maa-maas, but what she did was to eat a couple of them."

"So that's why you missed the meeting?"

"Precisely. I mean, I suppose you could say that. Actually, we brought in another dog."

"Ewedawg II?"

"Thought about that. No, her name is Lamdawg."

"You replaced Ewedawg with Lamdawg and that's why you missed the meeting?"

"Not exactly. You see, Lamdawg had been doing this line of work longer, and she was supposed to correct Ewedawg's behavior."

"Leadersheep?"

"Kind of. But, it didn't work, because Lamdawg did not believe in it. She figured we're all doomed to repeat our past transgressions."

"Like missing important meetings."

"Sometimes. Let me suggest to you that there's more to life than attending all meetings."

"There are baa-baas."

"Maa-maas. There comes a time when the sheep are calling you home."

"You've got to be kidding."

"No, I'm not kidding. Would I do that? Speaking of kids, did I ever tell you how much smarter goats are than sheep?"

"Spare me."

"And spoil the kid? Look, some people golf, some fish, some hunt, some poker, some tennis, some bridge, some drink, some paint, some garden, some gallivant."

"You sheep?"

"Exactly."

"Well, if you think you're going to sheep on this job, you've got another maa-maa coming–uh–what happened to Ewedawg?"

"See, that's how it works. Takes hold of you and won't turn loose. I'm sorry to say Ewedawg is gone."

"Gone? As in really gone?"

"I'm afraid so. Lamdawg ran her off, and I suppose Ewedawg said enough is enough, I'm leaving. She's probably out there somewhere on a cloud, maybe, protecting another shepherd's flock."

"Gee, I hope she's all right. I mean, I hope she didn't act like she was going to kill something, and somebody shot her."

"I know. I hope she's all right, too. I have this feeling that she's out there looking for a home, somewhere."

"If she comes back, would you give me a call?"

"You?"

"Yes."

"But you've got all those meetings to attend. You don't have time to be a shepherd. You don't like maa-maas. You like meetings."

"What meetings?"

*David*

# PHIL

$\mathcal{W}$hen Punxsutawney Phil saw his shadow, I turned in the four-wheel drive and said to my friend Edgar, "What does that *whistle* pig know about another six weeks of winter?"

Edgar and I agreed, some groundhogs, woodchucks, and *whistle pigs* might be as good as some of the two-legged weather forecasters we endure. As our Hardin County friend Willis Willyard said recently with regard to the forecasters, "Listen to 'em, then look up."

Edgar and I went off laughing and bragging about El Niño bringing us as many unseasonably warm conditions in February as any farmers had a right to imagine.

As it turns out, Punxsutawney Phil must've been to Berlitz. He must've translated a thing or two from El Niño, which had somehow not come to our attention. Something like *sitiado por la nieve: **Snowbound!***

It started snowing on a Tuesday night, and it acted as if it didn't know when to stop. We're not sure whether Phil or El Niño sent it.

Didn't matter. What did matter was that some varmint up in the thicket alongside the Bunker Hill Road could've bitten into our electric wire. Or something

87

fell on it. Who knows?

"David, do you all have power down there?" neighbor Pete wanted to know on the telephone in his house on top of the hill.

"No, we don't, do you?"

"Nope."

"Let me know when you do."

We did have ice cold running water. And we did have the telephone to keep company with Pete and his wife, Boots, and the rest of the world, but beyond that we were getting deeper and deeper into snow. Reminded me some of the winter of '50. El Niño and Phil must've been playing the fool then, too.

I brought in wood and coal for the fireplace in the bedroom, and we started closing doors to shut off the rest of this 150-year-old house. The temperature had dropped to somewhere in the twenty-degree vicinity and the snow was headed to somewhere in the twenty-*inch* depth. That can be a losing combination on any gambling boat.

Edgar came by in his four-wheel, and we went to check on the twin calves we'd brought to the barn lot the day before the snowstorm. They looked gaunt, and they were beginning to double up.

"Don't believe they'll make it."

"Don't believe so."

We bottle-fed the newborns again because the mama cow was more interested in being back with the herd. Sometimes Mother Nature has a definite mind of her own.

The second day of the snow, the heifer twin died.

We decided to chance it and take the mama cow and the other twin, a bull calf, back to the herd. If we didn't, mama was going to cowdoze through snow-sagged fences. We placed the calf on some trampled-down hay in the field. (Beware of trying to wrestle half-ton cows into warm stalls during a snowstorm.) The first thing the mother cow did was to get into a head-knocking contest with two other cows that must have decided that cow-*out*-of-the-herd does not automatically equal cow-welcomed-*back*-to-the-herd. Mother Nature again. Maybe. Might've been one of those I'm-home-again-and-so-why-don't-you-all-love-me-like-you-used-to things.

On the third day the bull calf died along with another newborn and the herd finally settled down comfortably in flank-deep snow. Edgar and I didn't see any reason to blame anybody for it–Punxsutawney Phil, El Niño,

Bad Luck, Mother Nature, the Mama Cows, or Ourselves. In the same way, we didn't blame Kentucky Rural Electric for our having no power in our house for two and a half days. Sometimes things like twenty inches of snow just happen, and we believe what you do is try to make the best of it and not waste precious, warm moments blaming somebody for it.

It turned out to be a good time to read Janice Holt Giles's *Hannah Fowler*. The way she and her husband survived that blizzard of the late eighteenth century in pioneer Kentucky was enough to make twenty inches of snow on Plum Lick look like sunlit beaches in the Caribbean.

Meantime, we cooked in the fireplace, ate by the fireplace, and slept by the fireplace. The daylight hours were on the short side, but I read some of Harlan Hubbard's *Payne Hollow Journal*. He and his wife, Anna, *chose* not to have power. I decided that Hannah Fowler would have accepted it in a heartbeat. And she probably would have stuck her head out the door the way my wife did on the third night, and she would have called across the drifted snow to the repairman on the pole: "Thanks, fellas!"

*David*

# STEWARDS

$\mathcal{S}$pring plowing has given spirits the lift they needed. Each year, thanks go up for another opportunity to work with the soil.

Laying the sod over is a clean feeling. Edgar's plow point and the glistening steel of his plowshares knifing through the warming loam are good for the soul. Being intimately involved in the conditions of the earth brings connections and understandings not likely otherwise.

The belief in our originating in the elements of the earth and eventually returning there gives plowing an especially human and spiritual meaning. It makes us care about safeguarding the soil that has too long eroded down the hills of the Commonwealth, carried by streams to silt the Mississippi Delta.

Each year we plow more carefully. There's no call to plant in the lower bottom again where last year the water stood long after the flash flood rolled through. This land becomes a hay field. The ridges need the growth of decades turning under, but we'll need to take special care to keep the slopes intact. Once a gully takes hold, it's almost impossible to put it back the way it once was.

What the plowed ground needs now is alternate freezing and thawing conditions, the better to prepare the soil for planting. City folks complain: "Kentucky's weather is too unpredictable"–"First it's cold, then it's hot"– "Why doesn't it make up its mind?"

The soil has a mind with sophisticated thinking to rival geniuses. What Edison or Einstein could withstand the onslaught of man's misuse of the countryside? What Morse or Marconi could maintain poise after centuries of upheaval of every sort? The soil holds on stubbornly with unmatched determination.

Stewards of the soil do better when they combine their best thinking with every ounce of energy at their command and use it cooperatively with the universal principles working in nature. Another slab of concrete is not the answer. Another roadway is not necessarily rational. Another bridge to span the hills, another deep cut through limestone–these aren't always justified. The land deserves more loving touches.

Agriculture–"the science, art and business of cultivating the soil"–is what makes defensible the concrete, the roads, and the bridges. The complication lies in the tendency to believe that a quicker means of transportation takes priority over the fundamental nature of human existence, the very reason for our being.

As Edgar's plow turns the furrows it's well to be reminded of the importance of farming to the common wealth. Each spring is a renewal of a commitment to keep the land close to heart and hand. Science, art, and business bind and shape the commitment. Philosophy is included. It helps to provide the satisfaction of knowing intimately where humankind begins and ends. Between these two landmarks are the living and the loving, which involve the immediacy of the present, the richness of the past, and the promise of the future.

*David*

# No Checks Today

The owner of the tobacco crop was in the field by eight a.m. The workers had not shown up. Something told the owner they were not going to show up. Maybe it was because at the end of the previous day he had asked them for their Social Security numbers.

The owner hooked one of the tobacco wagons to the pickup truck because the tractor was in town for repairs. He worked alone, piling the sticks of tobacco on the wagon. Then he climbed up and moved the burley to the back of the wagon. Down again, pile again, move again. Loading heavy burley tobacco is not a job for one person.

The owner looked up about half past nine and saw four workers walking toward him. By the tone of their voices it was easy to tell there was something wrong.

"You all here to work today?" asked the owner.

"You find out anything about that tax?" replied one of the men.

"Yes, I found out that the tax has to be paid. The deduction has to be taken, and I have to match it–even if you don't pay, I have to pay yours and mine."

"That's not fair."

"That's the law."

"Can't you pay cash?"

"That would just be a way of trying to get around the law."

One of the workers had jumped up on the wagon and seemed ready to go to work, even if it meant disclosing his Social Security number. The other three remained on the ground, and it was clear to the owner that what one did, all four would do. One of the three men by the side of the wagon said he had a medical problem.

"You understand my position?" he said.

"No, I don't. You have to argue your medical problem with the right people."

"That's not fair," said the man, who at this point seemed childlike.

"Maybe it's not fair, but that's the way it is, and I'm not going to get into trouble with the tax people."

The conversation was just about finished. The men stared at the ground. They looked up in short glances. The man who had jumped up onto the wagon jumped back down again. The owner looked at the tobacco sticks. He looked at the sky. Drizzle was turning to bigger drops of rain. The ethical question was whether to break the law and house tobacco. Or leave the field and let it rain.

"Would you be so good as to unhook the wagon?" said the owner, whose mind was decided. One of the men pulled the pin. The rain fell, softly. The field was becoming oozy. The pickup truck moved through it. The men walked through it. The owner parked his pickup truck by the side of the house and went inside. The four tobacco workers left in their car. The owner called two accountants to verify his understanding of the situation.

"You can avoid the tax if you're dealing with contractors," said one of the accountants.

"They're anything but contractors," said the owner.

"It's a tough situation," said the accountant.

The owner went out to meet the tractor when the repair shop returned it. He took the tractor to the field, hooked up the wagon of tobacco, took it to the barn, and hung the tobacco himself.

It was a day no checks would be written.

*David*

93

# THE MELLOWING PROCESS

It's most noticeable after turning off Bunker Hill Road onto Plum Lick.

The foliage on the driver's side of the road is the first sign of the gradual shift of seasons. Even in early August the leaves are in their greenish-yellow stage, which means one thing. In only a few weeks it'll be September again, and by then most of the green will be replaced as the autumnal equinox approaches.

"A time or period of maturity verging on decline" may be a definition acceptable to some, but for two Plum Lickers there's no "decline."

You have to look for the positive in this seasonal alteration; otherwise despair damages the human spirit. The movie *Steel Magnolias* illustrates the real meaning of the annual shift toward cold and frozen winter days. Life goes on.

The leaves of summer, slowly losing their greenness as their supply of life-giving chlorophyll shuts down, become the stuff of which new generations are created. Neither leaf nor mankind should find despair in that.

Another sign is in the wood stored behind the meat house. It's time to bring it closer to the back door where it'll be dry for the annual celebration of the lighting of the first fire on the bedroom hearth in another autumn. This wood was once a tree with life abounding. Soon it will be ascending heavenward.

Days, and especially nights, have become cooler with the freshness of the changing air currents. A light comforter feels deliciously pleasant to tired souls.

At the end of summer, toppers of tobacco felt the breeze as it replaced the heat caught in the rows of towering burley tobacco. It came as balm, soothing and healing the sweating arms and hands that reached for flowering blooms and long, deep green suckers shooting upward.

The cattle have begun leaving the woods during the day, their refuge less needed now. The cows and calves are among the first to realize the scorch of summer is slowly shifting toward cooler moments.

From time to time, the sheep, heads bent low to avoid the sun of July, are beginning to look up in August. The cycle of estrus is starting, and the Dorset ram looks longingly through the gate, biding his time, hoping.

"I don't dream of Florida in winter," says a farmer to a visitor from Georgia who remains disbelieving. "To me, the joy of Kentucky is to witness the changing of the seasons. We have four here. None is too brutal to withstand, nor are they so long as to be a burden."

The miracle of Kentucky lies mainly in the loveliness of the seasonal movement. It is a treasure that is real. Perhaps a little marker for a leaf that has yellowed and fallen might read: "Here lies one who thrived in summer, who departed in autumn, so that others might come to taste the bounty of the good earth."

*David*

# A QUIET KENTUCKIAN

Debra T. Salsman
Sonora, Kentucky

Dear Ms. Salsman:

In the eight years I've been writing "The View from Plum Lick" in the *Kentucky Living* magazine, I've never received such a lovely and powerful letter as the one you wrote to me on July 17, 1997.

You and your late father and your love for him, your return with your son to school, all the memories and the hopes for the future and your clarity and sincerity of expression cause me to know that writing this monthly column is one of the most important, fulfilling things I do in this autumn time of my life. Thank you for the sharing.

Surely, others should be included in the harvest. Therefore, I'm requesting your permission to allow me to reprint your letter–each word of it–in my next column for *Kentucky Living*.

What you have written will encourage and inspire others.

Sincerely,

David Dick

The next time somebody scoffs and says, "There are no 'quiet Kentuckians,'" I'll smile and remember the letter that came in this past summer from a lady over in Sonora.

"Dear Sir:

"Every month 'The View from Plum Lick' is the first thing I read in *Kentucky Living*, and I always enjoy your articles. Two articles, though, have had special meaning for me. Please allow me a few minutes of your time to tell you what they've meant to me.

"The January, 1996, article, 'The Quiet Kentuckians' reduced me to tears the first time I read it. My father, one of those quiet Kentuckians, had been killed a few days earlier in a farm accident.

"The shock was wearing off and I was looking for ways to cope with the situation we had been left. There were no answers in your article, but it guided me to a way to look at my father's life and at my memories.

"I grew up on a small family farm, a not particularly successful farm; my mother had a job 'in town' and we always knew she worked because we needed the money. Granny was our child care provider (until I was old enough for the job), but my father was always where we could find him if we needed him.

"From him we learned much about work and pride, independence and self-reliance, frustration and determination. A high school dropout, he encouraged his children–there are four of us–in education.

"He received his GED when he was 66 years of age, two years before he died. I don't expect I'll meet many men more unassuming than he. His talents were many; his boasts about them few.

"He led a rather ordinary life; not always satisfied with it, but never giving up on it. He loved playing guitar, rebuilding guns, UK basketball, the Cincinnati Reds and The Courier-Journal.

"After he retired from farming he dropped his CJ subscription because of the expense. I bought the paper every day and at night either my youngest son or I would take it to him so he could read it before he went to bed.

"I took him the paper the night before he died, the last time I saw him alive.

"I believe he was not only a quiet Kentuckian but also quite a Kentuckian.

"'The Quiet Kentuckians' went into my keep folder where it has been joined by last month's article 'How Now....'

"When it became impossible to avoid discovering myself and the whys, at the age of 42 I enrolled in our community college to get the degree I've always wanted but have been afraid to attempt. (It remains to be seen how Governor Patton's higher education reform will affect this process but that's another story.)

"This fall my 19 year old son and I will be in the same history class; a situation I think may yield many discoveries. I want to work with abused women to help them find ways out, to help them discover.

"I want to write. I don't think I'll ever be finished asking why.

"I apologize for rambling on so in my effort to say thank you. In my discovery quest, I believe I need to find brevity.

> Thank you, sir.
> Very truly yours,
> Debra Salsman
> Sonora, Kentucky"

Dear Ms. Salsman:

Thank you for writing to me. Your letter makes everything worthwhile.

From Sonora to Plum Lick it's a distance of about 135 miles, but you and I have built us a bridge of understanding. And we're sharing it with others.

We've connected through this publication, *Kentucky Living*. Without it we might never have exchanged new ideas first-hand.

You've brought to life such qualities as respect for parents, respect for children and respect for our selves. You've drawn your strength from a family farm that survived by coming to terms with urban realities.

You've identified the essential concept of putting discovery ahead of construction.

We know if all we do is keep building with the same old blocks of time and circumstance, never allowing for new possibilities, we vegetate and fossilize and miss the richness that comes with growth.

You've not renounced the past. You've held it dearly in your memory.

You've not distrusted the future. You've joined your son in a new generation of discovery.

You say you want to write. Well, I encourage you to do what every quiet Kentuckian should do. Keep a little journal. Keep it for yourself and for posterity. Each page will make a better building block in your new life. I started to say "career," but I like the word "life" much more.

Sincerely,

David Dick

# DROUGHT TIME

*I*n the dusty autumn of 1987, the wells were still pumping in the bottomland in front of the Isaac Shelby Crouch house where I live in my sixth-generation stubbornness. Despite the drought in every direction, drawing tighter and tighter like a hangman's noose, these wells are producing precious, life-sustaining water. Each night before retiring we've been offering thanks to the Father of All Waters.

The #1 well, which came in at thirty-eight feet below the surface, and the #2 well, which came in at about seventy-eight feet are all that are standing between us and having to sell off all our livestock just at a time when we're trying to build up our herd.

The #3 well, which came in at about eighty-nine feet below the surface a little farther down on the bank of Plum Lick Creek, does not have a pump installed in it because the water is salty and it probably should be used only as a last resort. That time may come sooner than we think, because Plum Lick Creek's bed is powder dry. Throughout this area of the state (northeast of Lexington about thirty miles as the crows fly) the drought has sucked the life out of most of our creeks. There are a few stagnant pools here and there, but mostly the waterways have become desolate ways.

We aren't used to this sort of thing. After all, this isn't West Texas, and it isn't Death Valley--at least it isn't supposed to be. Maybe this Kentucky drought will toughen us, and maybe it'll cause more of us to do as Booker T. Washington said: "Put your bucket down where you are."

All of us can't do that. If Great-grandfather John and his brother, Isaac, had only known that only thirty-eight feet beneath their feet there was so much water! Enough for one hundred head of cows and their calves, a small flock of sheep, a few meat hogs, and enough water to run the Big House and irrigate the garden. If they'd only known, the wells would have been dug more than a century ago.

They relied upon "never-failing" springs. We did too until we came to the conclusion that the last earth tremors here must've altered the pathways of the "never-failing" springs. It proved once again that nothing is forever or never failing. In any event, the current drought has finished sealing off this normal supply of water. As for the cistern beside our house, it's like an old bottle collecting dust in some corner of the stock barn. Dry leaves fill the gutters of the old 1850 house, groaning with the nightly wind blowing in from the scorched hillsides. Not a tear falls from the sullen sky because, as one old Texan used to put it, "It don't hardly ever rain during a drought."

The seventy-eight-foot-deep well is there as a backup to the #1 water supply, and we've offered it to some of our neighbors for their livestock. This water has a sulfuric content, making it unsuitable for human consumption, but it could made a crucial difference for livestock when we get down to serious crawdad time. There's an ethical question here too. How much should we charge for water in the depths of a drought? More than we might when rainfall is plentiful? We think the answer is fairly obvious. We don't charge anything.

A drought is a time for helping friends and neighbors, not an opportunity for gouging them. We realize that some folks make a living selling water, and we don't have a problem with that. But that's not how we make our living, and we see this as a friendly time to share some of our God-given good fortune.

We didn't make the water. We didn't put it here. We were just blessed enough to be inspired one day to see if we could possibly find it. A couple of years ago we obtained aerial maps of this section of Plum Lick Creek, and we took them to John Thrailkill, a geologist at the University of Kentucky. He studied them, and he said, "Do you see where this runoff makes a perpendicular juncture with the creek? Drill there, and if you don't hit water within seventy-five feet, pull up and drill again anywhere within one hundred feet of the first location."

We didn't have to try a second time. We hit the water at thirty-eight feet and the volume was extraordinary. How could there be that much water so near the surface? We'd give our eyeteeth to be able to see a topographical cross-section of the #1 well to see how wide and deep the underground stream really is. Did we hit a stream, or did we luck upon an underground lake? You never know until you put your bucket down.

The trouble often is that we wait for somebody else to do all our bucketing for us, and when there's a serious drought our normal source may not be enough. That's why a few years ago when we were asked if we wanted "city water" piped to us along Plum Lick Road I said, "No thank you." (Later, when the local water association received permission to build the line, we tapped in because my wife said there was no sense in cutting off our nose to spite our thirst.)

It wasn't pigheadedness, I like to think, that caused me to make the original decision. It was based on the Crouch family belief that there's something just a mite illogical about damming up surface water miles away, flooding good farmland, then laying down pipe that can't convey any more water than what falls out of the sky and accumulates in the impoundment.

It isn't original with me when I say, for many folks, that water isn't water unless it's either dammed up someplace or coming out of a spigot in the kitchen sink. Even in a drought we're literally standing above millions of gallons of water waiting to be tapped. This is groundwater–water in the ground, not on top of it. Maybe there deserves to be a different name for it. Instead of groundwater we could call it God's lagoon, or creation's moisture, or eternity's treasure.

Whatever we call it, it's different from surface runoff. It's deep. It's true. It'll sustain us when the creeks run proverbially dry and the dams look like what they are–concrete barriers. But we're not taking anything for granted, and we're not so bold as to brag about our good fortune. There may come a day when one of our wells fails to produce. That's why it's important to have backups–more wells drilled to the right level at the right place. That takes money, but during an extreme drought, as we're in now, a producing well is priceless. God helps those who help themselves by putting their bucket down where they are.

We're in neither the water selling business nor the water well drilling business. We're in the survival business. And we're guided by an idea that was shared with me by Liz Shear, in the University of Kentucky School of Journalism. She quoted her father: "All the water that was here in the beginning is still here; and all the water that's here now is all the water there ever will be."

*David*

# EDGAR

*I*t was not Robert Frost who said, "Good fences make good neighbours." It was the "old-stone savage" who said it.

> He only says, "Good fences make good neighbours."
> Spring is the mischief in me, and I wonder
> If I could put a notion in his head:
> "Why do they make good neighbours? Isn't it
> Where there are cows? But here there are no cows...."

Yes, this is true and there is a time and a place for a fence or a wall and a time and a place for mending one.

I learned some valuable lessons from Edgar Lovell. He's younger and stronger than I am and more knowledgeable than Robert Frost or "The Hired Man" or I am when it comes to putting a gate into a fence to help control the cows and maintain the hay field in a more orderly way.

It's time for a little test. We'll make it the multiple-choice kind, since that seems to be so popular these days in institutions of higher learning. Essay questions aren't cool.

Question: What do you do first, high up on the hill, when you need a gate where there hasn't been one since some ancestral "old-stone savage armed" strung out the fence dividing the property, keeping out or keeping in everything in a legal and practical way (to check the cows and sometimes to pacify warring members of the human family)?

   a. cut the fence

   b. pull out the old rusted staples
      (sometimes, farther north, pronounced "steeples")

   c. nail in the new shiny staples

   d. dig holes for new posts

   e. none of the above

Answer: None of the above.

The first thing you do is test the posts to see if they're rotten. They probably are. The #9 wire is probably holding up the posts instead of the posts holding up the wire.

So you leave the fence the way it is and go looking for a locust tree that's not doughy pronounced doe-dee (not to be confused with doughty), soft at the core. This is good because it makes you better acquainted with bestowed blessings upon the land.

You note the black walnut trees and observe that this year's crop looks promising. The squirrels won't mind if you come back later for a burlap sack full for putting in the driveway where the farm vehicles will hull them for you. The cracking of the shells comes later this winter when the cold winds are blowing and you need a little something to challenge your mind and your knobby fingers.

You comment upon the papaw thicket and discuss the merits of sitting down and eating one of the mushy fruits. (Remember one of the courtin' songs of your youth: "Picking up papaws, pat 'em on the po-po"?)

Edgar and I spot a locust that looks just about right. We take a minute to talk about it. It requires no committee approval. There are no stockholders involved, no boards of trustees or visitors. Edgar uses the chainsaw to bring the tree down, and he measures off two posts seven and a half feet long. We load them into the back of the pickup truck, and I count the rings of growth at the base of the tree. It took twenty-five years to manufacture what we needed for our own mending wall.

True or False: Now you cut the fence?

False. If you did that, as noted earlier, the whole thing would probably creel over (lose its delicate balance...We have to use a spell!).

The first thing you do is to use fencing pliers to pull out the old staples.

Then you push aside the rotten posts, or let them fall, and dig the holes deeper for the freshly-cut locust posts. The holes should be two and a half feet deep, leaving five feet above ground. Then you drive in the new, shiny staples.

Now can we cut the dern fence?

Yes, you may. But be sure to leave twelve inches or more from the post out to where the cut is made. This gives you extra support by wrapping the ends of the wire (after cutting the two inner panels) and hammering the excess into the post. Be careful when you cut the wire that it doesn't fly back and hit you in the eye or make a mark on your face. You're ugly enough as it is.

Roll up the fence panel and put in the store-bought gate (a home-made wire gap is all right, but it takes longer and sometimes it's more practical to buy something from the store, because those folks have to live too). Wire it until you have time to install snags (metal points augured into the posts for hinges).

As Edgar and I head back down the hill, we don't talk about poetry and we don't feel like "old-stone savages armed." Robert Frost and we know that good fences with handy gates make better behaving cows, and if relations among neighbors are improved in the process, so much the better.

*David*

# LIGHT

"*H*i! How're you feeling?"

She looks at me.

"Well, that's all right. You seem to be coming along just fine."

She blinks.

"Here, let me bring you some water and a little something to eat."

Her eyes fix more intently on me. I move on down the line past the children and the two elderly ladies who have moved in with them. "Good to see you all having such a good time this Christmas season. I've got some goodies for you."

I walk slowly through the crowd on the other side. "Good evening. How're you doing? You're looking fine. Nice to have you all here together on this cold night in December. Christmas will be here before we know it."

No one speaks. But all eyes are on me. I walk carefully so as not to disturb my flock of sheep.

I go back to the water faucet, turn it on past its usual drip, and use the garden hose to fill the bucket in the first stall. The first ewe, expected to lamb any time now, comes over and sips. I scoop up a pan full of ground corn and set it beside the bucket of water. The ewe, making signs of twins or better, nibbles gratefully. I scoop another panful of ground corn and spread it in the trough for the late lambs and two old ewes I'm trying to save for at least another season. The oldest and boniest old girl, her ears frozen by two-thirds during last winter's blast, is beginning to warm up again. The shot of medicine I gave her three nights ago seems to be working. If I can save this scrawny, doleful ovine scrap, I can probably rescue anything.

Once I've filled the big bucket with ground corn I take it over to the crowd of fifty-two healthy ewes, all in their various stages of lamb birth. I knee my way to the improvised trough along the south wall of the lambing shed. The feeding frenzy begins. Up in the loft I pick my way along the path created by the daily removal of bales of hay. Above the crowd I drop manna from heaven–a very fine feeling, pleasing a crowd so much. As each loop of binder twine is removed, it's saved and looped within easy reach for future use. It's a handy and practical substitute for manufactured hinges and nails, as the four-by-four nurseries are built when needed.

When everybody is fed and settled in for the night, it's pure pleasure to stand there in the middle of the barn, forearms resting on the top board of the pens, watching the Christmas crowd milling about, shopping for morsels.

Tommy Mason has been down to talk about installing the warm-water trough. That'll make everything so much more convenient, especially the breaking of ice on coldest mornings. "I'd also like some extra light over there, maybe four more outlets for bulbs." Tommy nodded.

I say "goodnight" to the sheep, turn off the lights, and close the barn door.

*David*

# GETTING UNDERSTANDING

"*M*en are like plants; the goodness and flavour of the fruit proceeds from the peculiar soil...in which they grow."

Words from the Letters of a Pennsylvania farmer to his friend in England in 1782 recall a time of simplicity, an era of innocence with roots deeply embedded in rich soil. Kentucky has such a heritage of unparalleled fertility. Without a healthy topsoil, no great civilization can survive. While concrete is essential for industrial growth, a community that smothers agriculture with endless parking lots will one day discover the folly of excess.

"When the severities of that season have dispirited all my cattle, no farmer ever attends them with more pleasure than I do; it is one of those duties which is sweetened with the most rational satisfaction. I amuse myself in beholding their different tempers, actions, and the various effects of their instinct now powerfully impelled by the force of hunger. I trace their various inclination, and the different effects of their passions, which are exactly the same as among men; the law is to us precisely what I am in my barn yard, a bridle and check to prevent the strong and greedy from oppressing the tame and weak..."

Letters from an American Farmer is the kind of book I'll be wanting to curl up with before a nice fire this winter. It's a slender volume, the sort that fits nicely in the palm of one hand.

"It is the folly of the world, constantly, which confounds its wisdom," said Oliver Wendell Holmes.

A joy, then, before a warm fire this winter in home sweet Kentucky, shall be the continuing search for wisdom. As it is written in Proverbs, "Wisdom is the principal thing." Yet there is no hope for wisdom without the soil. It sustains the elements of life.

*David*

# JENNY

"*We* hope we're not keeping you from something you really need to do," I said as she ushered me through her comfortable country home filled with family pictures.

"Oh," laughed Virginia Wiche, "we're always busy here."

As we sat and chatted on the high rear deck that faces the lake, a flock of Canadian geese in V-formation floated in for a landing.

"They reside here all year long, much to our dismay. All the tops of the green beans are eaten off and Jeneen says it's the geese." Jeneen is Jenny and Fred Wiche's youngest daughter.

What does professional gardener Fred think of that?

"He says we're probably right."

While he taped his weekly television program, Jenny and I settled into a conversation about what it's really like being Fred Wiche's wife and how they came to settle here in Shelby County.

"We used to live in a subdivision and we had a little place where we raised potatoes, tomatoes, beans–but when Barney Arnold [at WHAS Radio] got sick and as Fred got more and more involved, I could tell he really liked the country.

"Our neighbor said, 'There's land next to me that's going up for sale.' So we came and looked it over, but Fred liked this one because he liked the lake and had the foresight to know that one day we'd have to do irrigation.

"We did all the landscaping, and we planted day lilies and that grove of trees." Jenny gestured over the beautiful, sloping yard toward the island they developed in the lake. Emerald green velvet is more what it looks like.

"This would never have happened if I hadn't wanted it to. I used to spend days and days mulching. I even laid the whole rock path down to the lake. I get out on the tractor and mow. Life's never boring when you live with Fred Wiche."

Fred and Jenny annually conduct garden tours to England and Ireland, and Toby Tours in Louisville books group visits to the Wiche property. When they arrive, Fred carefully explains the attributes of each tree and flower. On Monday and Friday mornings, forty to fifty people show up and oldest daughter Teal caters lunch.

"So many people just come to sit and enjoy the peace and quiet," says Jenny.

"We're not farmers. We don't have cattle, just trees and plants. My favorite flower? Probably the roses. I have a rose garden. Double Delight is my favorite. Magnolias, dogwoods, and redbuds are my favorite trees."

Jenny was the eighth of twelve children. There were Fannie Mae, Charles Thomas, Ilean, Evangeline, Ruth, Porter, Mary Elizabeth and Virginia (Jenny). They came along without fanfare, but on February 23, 1941, there appeared Beulah, John, Mildred, and Martine, better known as the Lashley Quads of Graves County.

"The quads were premature, and Yellow Cab sent a cab down to take my mother and the babies to the hospital," said Jenny. "The Carnation Company gave them a contract and the Binghams would give them birthday parties."

"My father was very protective of the quads. He built a big house that had four big windows in the front, and he charged people to come peek in the window at the babies. I remember a picture of me standing on the porch and sucking on my finger. So much attention was for them that I just went off somewhere and read a book."

Jenny's mother died when she was forty-three. "She died when I was five and a half and the quads were three...I never really knew my mother, but I vaguely remember her sitting by the wood stove. She always looked older than my father, and I think she was not well when she had the quads."

"My father never remarried....We milked cows, fed the chickens, cleaned out the chicken house, and carried water to the men when they were bailing hay. We were responsible for cooking all the meals for the farm laborers. Father wished he had more sons, but he had all these girls," Jenny laughed.

"My father never believed in college education. He thought that we should all just get married and have children," said Jenny, who was determined not to follow the path of so many farm girls before her. "I graduated as valedictorian from Leitchfield High School....I went to Bowling Green College of Commerce....After graduation I came to Louisville and got a job with Brown-Foreman and was asked by the National Guard if I'd represent them in a beauty contest."

On a Sunday afternoon at Bowman Field, Jenny Lashley won a lot more than just a beauty contest. She won the heart of a young WHAS reporter who was covering the contest.

As many of Fred Wiche's friends know, last year he was diagnosed with prostate cancer, the same disease that comes to so many men, including my own husband.

"Fred's illness makes moments more precious. We spend more time together. We take walks together. Fred had never been sick and all of a sudden, 'boom.' The only good thing I can say about this is that I see more of Fred.

"Fred loves what he's doing and he's been so happy. That's what's important," Jenny says with a smile.

As I leave her place of places (she calls it her Valhalla), the Canadian geese rise up again from the lake. Summer moves toward fall–Jenny and I agree–one more precious day at a time.

*Lalie*

# FRED

$\mathcal{T}$he Cathedral of the Assumption in downtown Louisville was full. They had to put out extra chairs. The organist's Prelude soared to the vaulted ceiling, where stars were painted on a light blue Heaven. And the final verse of "Amazing Grace" rose mightily:

*When we've been there ten thousand years,*
*bright shining as the sun,*
*we've no less days to sing God's praise*
*than when we'd first begun.*

Fred Wiche was a gracious, humble, and simple man, endlessly kind with marvelous loyalty, a great teacher who walks now with God in the garden.

By such tributes are angels sometimes described.

Shyly and softly, Fred would be the first to smile and to laugh, for he never seemed to take himself seriously. He was as natural to creation as wild geese in synchronized flight, pausing to rest on a small Shelby County farm before heading home.

I first met Fred thirty-nine years ago in the tiny WHAS newsroom. He'd already been there a year and knew his way to City Hall, the Jefferson County Courthouse, the police station, the fire department, the hotels where the famous and the not so famous came to their favorite watering holes. As a cub reporter, an English literature major of all things, I knew nothing of professional journalism, and Fred was a kind and patient co-worker.

Fred and I were broadcast journalists in what we like to think were the glory days. It was the time when Harry Truman shook our hand and scolded us for not reading the Constitution of the United States of America. John Kennedy and Richard Nixon came to town, and they fanned the fervor of the riverfront crowds. It was the time when the DuPont explosion rocked the city. And the terrible day would dawn when John Kennedy would be memorialized in this same Cathedral of the Assumption.

You know, it's really easy to make sense out of Fred Wiche's death, especially his, because we don't remember him for breaking stories about the purchase of the Belle of Louisville or the latest decisions of the Kentucky State Fair Board. Rather than remember him at all, we actually see him in a profusion of day lilies.

Fred had the good sense to stop chasing fire trucks early enough in his career to become Everyman's weekend gardener. "He walks with God in the garden," eulogized Dr. John Wesley Slider, pastor of Saint Mark United Methodist Church. Dr. Slider went on to describe God's first meeting with Fred in Heaven, putting His arm across his shoulder and saying, "I've got this little problem with this tree over here."

Wrongly, I had thought that the Cathedral of the Assumption would be bedecked with flowers on June 22, 1998, for "A Celebration of the Life of Fred Wiche." No, Fred most likely didn't want it that way, and lovely Virginia respected his wishes. Splendidly, she accompanied her husband's coffin into a place where remembrance was adorned with the living—Fred's daughters, other family members, and so many friends representing untold thousands of those who never hesitated or feared to say, "Fred, I've got this little problem with this blooming plant."

The lesson I've learned from Fred is that now you'll find him in the flowers of thousands of gardens throughout the Commonwealth, most especially in my own. I believe it tells me that I must be self-reliant. First, I must teach myself, then I must teach others by the example of my own good garden. Reverend Slider said, "It would be good to have Fred for one more day, but it's best that he now walks with God."

After Bob Hill's earthy tribute to his longtime friend, after Jennifer Hartlage's sweet singing of "Ave Maria" and "Hymn of Promise," there will always remain the words of Fred's favorite lines of poetry read by a young man for his "Uncle Fred."

*Do not stand at my grave and weep;*
*I am not there. I do not sleep.*
*I am a thousand winds that blow;*
*I am the diamond glints of snow.*
*I am the sunlight on ripened grain;*
*I am the gentle autumn's rain.*
*When you awaken in the morning hush;*
*I am the swift uplifting rush,*
*Of quiet birds in circled flight.*
*I am the soft star that shines at night.*
*Do not stand at my grave and cry.*
*I am not there: I did not die.*

(Author Unknown)

And true enough, when I awoke the morning after "A Celebration of the Life of Fred Wiche," a light rain was falling, and I thought of him again.

*David*

114

# TIMOTHY TAYLOR

On July 4, 1999, Timothy Taylor will be eighty-one years upon the earth, the good earth.

His body has worn remarkably well (he has an artificial heart valve). He treats it with the same respect as he does the beloved grassland upon which he lives in McCreary County. You can find him there in the midst of magnificent trees. He roams with his wife, Peg, and their border collie, Clyde, beneath the tulip poplar, oak, hemlock, sweet gum, dogwood, mountain magnolia, cedar, hickory, walnut, persimmon, and pine.

To Timothy, a tree is not just a tree; it's a sustainable, renewal resource each with its own purpose. Timothy is not in favor of wasting anything. And he's not in favor of standing around doing nothing. This year alone he has planted one thousand trees.

He points to one of the true giants seeded long before his time, an American beech, probably four hundred years old. The notches on the towering behemoth mark the boundary where public land ends and private ownership begins. Some such trees, Timothy explains, have been known to make a thousand fine doors for houses.

Anybody who thinks the slim man with the shock of white hair isn't spry ought to try following Timothy Taylor through the Daniel Boone National Forest. On a Sunday afternoon, he wants his visitors to experience a hidden waterfall on Rock Branch creek, another essential part of the ecology of man and his surroundings. Along the way we savor the intricate delights of lady's slippers and discuss the possibilities of partridge peas.

Lifelong teachers, Timothy and Peg live nearby in a 126-year-old log cabin. Presently, she's Director of the McCreary Center of Somerset Community College. He's retired from the University of Kentucky College of Agriculture but continues to consult.

My wife and daughter and I sit with Tim and Peg beneath a shady plum tree in the front yard of their Good Spring Farm where, literally, weeds don't dare to grow.

Most of his life, Timothy Taylor has been a scholar of grass and legumes–bluegrass, orchard grass, clover, alfalfa, tall fescue, and, of course, timothy! It is the grasslands working with the woodlands that provide life for human beings for thousands of years. "We as practical people need to harvest trees. It is my practice to replant and nurture the forest," says Timothy.

Student and teacher at Cornell, Penn State, and the University of Kentucky, Dr. Taylor "retired" in 1985 to the place where he was born near Cumberland Falls.

A book cries out to be written about all this and, maybe, Timothy will get around to finishing his manuscript.

But, there's so much to do, and Timothy Taylor can't seem to resist doing it. There's the kitchen garden to be kept just right so that Peg need take only a few steps outside the back door to gather in lettuce, tomatoes, and prize asparagus. There are the seven beef cows, the bull, and Peg's riding mare, Molly, to be rotated among five small pastures, each lush with grass that causes animals to know a good thing when they chew it.

Past his great-great-grandfather's millstone at the swinging garden gate, past the water barrel where the goldfish control the mosquitoes, past his father's sourwood walking stick leaning against the front door, inside this small cabin of hand-hewn tulip poplars, are books in all directions.

In the sunroom where two pairs of binoculars are constantly available for bird watching, there's a mini-arsenal of books: *Kentucky Birds, The Audubon Society Field Guide to North American Birds, Eastern Region, Weeds of Kentucky and Adjacent States, The Audubon Society Field Guide to North American Insects & Spiders, Trees & Shrubs of Kentucky,* and *Peterson's Field Guide, Eastern Birds.*

Timothy Taylor's byword, which could be a password for many who care about heritage and the future: "I try to do the things that I judge to be important."

Timothy's words can be interpreted many ways. The challenge in understanding his fundamental values lives in simple, grassroots reality.

*David*

# LITTLE REDS

*P*ioneers stood on Jeptha Knob, the highest elevation in Shelby County, and they believed they'd found Paradise. According to tradition, that's how Mt. Eden, Kentucky, got its name, symbolic of a Promised Land.

Kenneth Tinsley lives on Main Street in Mt. Eden, more or less straddling the Shelby-Spencer County line. Mr. Tinsley is eighty-three years old. In his younger years he "clerked in stores," sang, and played the piano. Mr. Tinsley says now he likes to read histories, and it was he who put his visitor on to the pioneers who gave Mt. Eden its name more than two centuries ago.

The simplicity and the rolling, rugged beauty of southern Shelby County (named in honor of Kentucky's first governor, Isaac Shelby) speaks today to a Commonwealth of 120 settled, maturing counties, from the mountains to the bottom lands of the Jackson Purchase.

Simplicity, yet rich variety, is a given in Kentucky, a gift pleasured by three and three-quarter million individuals.

The cultural composite includes eighty-five-year-old Marvin Perry, living with his wife, Virginia, on the edge of Mt. Eden. Mrs. Perry hallooed for her husband down at the barn, but he didn't answer. He was quietly trimming the fore-lock of his twenty-year-old mare, Nell. "She's made me more money than anything else

on the farm–nine walking horse foals."

Mr. Perry agreed to take his visitor to show him something rarely if ever discovered by travelers breezing along on the interstates and the parkways: Kentucky's third Red River.

Most have heard of the famous Red River Gorge in Powell County. Fewer know of the Red River flowing north out of Tennessee into Simpson County, then crossing into Logan County before looping back into Tennessee.

Kentucky's third Red River is only about two miles long, the only known "river" that empties into a creek, Little Beech Creek, near the Shelby-Spencer-Anderson County lines.

The oddity illustrates several realities about the Kentucky gift of the summer of 1998: there are many discoveries just waiting to be made; and you never know how many good people you'll meet when you go looking.

An artist and her husband, Catherine and Kenneth Tuggle, live up the third Red River. Formerly of Louisville, they represent what Ivan Potter of Shelby County calls "a redefinition of community to a scale they can live with and control."

Ivan and his wife, Mary, operate Proud Mary's Booksellers in Shelbyville. He sums up the new Kentucky experience as "shutting out the noises of life."

The third Red River (no one has remembered how such a little stream of water grew up to become a "river") is the quintessential murmur of simple Kentucky living. Oh yes, flash floods occur and visitor beware, but, taken as a whole, the waters running down from Cat Ridge empty eventually into Beech Creek to become one of the sources of Taylorsville Lake.

There are more than three thousand acres in Taylorsville Lake, just one of the forty-nine state parks and approximately sixty wildlife management areas in Kentucky, believed to have more miles of streams than any other state (with the exception of Alaska, which defies most comparisons).

Bass, trout, perch, and catfish in a variety of species inhabit other major impoundments and their tributaries: Dale Hollow, Green River Lake, Kentucky Lake, Lake Barkley, Lake Cumberland, Rough River Lake, and many more. (A valuable guide is Delorme's best-selling *Kentucky Atlas & Gazetteer*.)

In *The Compleat Angler*, Izaak Walton describes fishing as "A moderator of passions, a procurer of contentedness."

*The Kentucky Encyclopedia*, published in this final decade of the twentieth century, cites a statewide poll conducted by *The Courier-Journal* in 1989: "Some 60 percent of those surveyed 'feel a sense of closeness to God daily.'"

It's not just the older folks, the Perrys and the Tinsleys of Mt. Eden, the Tuggles who've decided that life is good on little Red Rivers, and the Potters and the Proud Marys of the small independent bookstores in the county seats.

It's the little boy who comes into the Mt. Eden Country Store and asks politely for a "baloney sandwich, plain" and tops it off with some candy. It's the young man standing in his front yard on Back Creek Road, politely answering the questions of a stranger.

But, truth to tell, there are few "strangers" in Kentucky, a friendly place to live and to thrive. And it seasons so well with time.

*David*

# NAKED TRUTH

"Agriculture" is a five-dollar word for the five-cent word that I prefer, which is "farming." At least "agriculture" is a better word than "agribusiness," which I consider an aggravation. But we may be stuck with it and might as well learn to live with it, along with some other fancy critters such as "agronomics" and "geoponics."

Call it what you will, about half the population of Kentucky is rural and the other half would be up that well-known tributary without a navigational mechanism if it were not for farmers who work from sunup to sundown seven days a week. All they do is produce the food and fiber without which we'd all be a bunch of hungry, naked jaybirds.

We may be farmers, but we aren't as lacking in sophistication as some may suppose. We're better educated, better motivated, more committed than we're generally given credit for being. We not only have votes to cast, we have publicly elected officials who go home at the end of a legislative day and start mowing back forties. Most of us have not declared holy war on city folks. We think it's dandy if they want to live high in the sky in perfect security and dine on chateaubriand—we just want the record to reflect where that good eatin' comes from. And when our friends in New York City dress up in one-hundred percent wool, we'd feel better knowing those fleeces came from right here in Kentucky.

The trouble is, too many city children (and a good many country children as well) have never known where milk or eggs come from, or where hamburgers and hotdogs come from. Farmers would like for everybody to understand that these products originate with real honest-to-goodness cows and real honest-to-goodness chickens cared for by real honest-to-goodness people of the land.

Farmers have sometimes earned well deserved reputations for being championship complainers and award-winning moaners and groaners. One reason we are the way we are is because we don't have the luxury of setting the price on what we sell, and we have no control over the price of what we buy. Some may be sick and tired of hearing about all this. But, if we weren't crazy enough to go out there 365 days of the year in blistering summer heat and bone-numbing winter cold and take care of the cows and chickens and turkeys and sheep and hogs and dogs, there you'd be in your urban heaven wondering where the next meal was coming from. That is, unless you think the twenty-first century is going to be all vitamin bottles and artificial yummies.

*David*

# MARVIN AND JANE

Mr. and Mrs. Marvin Douglas
Kings Mountain, Kentucky

Dear Marvin and Jane:

May we first-name you now? It seems right. We hope we'll be David, Lalie, and Ravy for you. But "Friends" is also good!

I came to my piled-high desk just now and played the game I sometimes do, when I'm tired, worn out with trying to be better organized: I reach in and take the first thing that finds my hand and I open it and read it. "Dear Friends" saved the day, a day that had been all right but now was winding down to the wearisome part.

You brought a smile where there'd been none. You lightened the load of my mental estate. Your letter was like no other that we've received in quite some time. So, thank you for writing and making me feel good about the world and the little role I play in it.

We'll be at Kentucky Crafted again this year. Did you say you were participating? I hope you'll be across from us again.

Thank you for your encouragement. My next book, *The Scourges of Heaven*, is at the University Press of Kentucky, and I'm now at work on *The Rivers of Kentucky*. According to my river map you're at the headwaters of the Green. You should be my authority on Hites Creek and Knob Lick Creek!

Warmest wishes for 1998 and all the other years to follow.

Sincerely,

David Dick

Jane and Marvin Douglas live on Grove Ridge Road, high on a hill above Yosemite in Casey County, about seven miles from Kings Mountain, Kentucky. (For those who've moved here from Yosemite, California, the way you pronounce Yosemite, Kentucky, is Yo-se-mite with the emphasis on the first and last syllables. Just thought you might want to know, if ever you're down this way and go asking for directions.)

With six children, all daughters (one set of twins), and twelve grandchildren, Jane and Marvin, you might want to say, have earned some time of their own to do what they want to do. Jane has been teaching business and accounting in high school for over thirty-eight years, and Marvin has spent just about all of his sixty-two years as a carpenter. He might qualify as one of the best either side of Yosemite, either way you pronounce it, any way you cut it down, stack it up, and put it together.

"How many nails have you driven in your lifetime, Marvin?" is a frequent question.

"Tons," is Marvin's standard answer.

He has built forty to fifty houses (that he remembers) including, naturally, the one where he and Jane now sit quietly among all the other wooden things created by this premier carpenter in his combination shop/garage. Out there amid a small forest of tools and lumber of every conceivable description, that no one else wanted, the motto is: "From Splinter to Splendor."

"I try to save every piece of wood," says Marvin, speaking with the softest of smiles on his kind, weathered face.

There's on the order of fifty little clock stands, which, Marvin says, Governor Patton will take with him to Japan. They'll be gifts from back home in Kentucky where expert craftsmanship is still alive and well, and they wouldn't be the same if they came off an assembly line. There's a market for both, but it sure is nice to have a choice.

There's the poplar wall hanger shaped like a ball glove with a place for the bat, the ball, and the cap. "It would make a nice birthday present for my grandchild who lives in Atlanta," I muse aloud. There are rows of miniature cedar, oak, and cherry boxes for calling cards, the four sides slotted as if they were meant to be. It takes a fine eye and a steady hand for that. Earlier this year, they were a big hit at Kentucky Crafted: The Market at the fairgrounds in Louisville, the same weekend that others were concentrating on basketball in the annual passion called "March Madness."

Down near Kings Mounting there's a different fever up where the wind blows with keenness, quickening the walk of a man and a woman in the closing minutes of their game.

There are coffee tree plaques of the outline of the Commonwealth of Kentucky, suitable for mounting clocks. "I like to see what I can do...I like to do the best I can," says Marvin Douglas, whose father, Edward, was also a carpenter. "It's the end of the line" for this branch of the family tree, though the daughters "don't wait on their husbands to put nails in the wall."

When the daughters were girls on Grove Ridge Road, they made their own doll furniture. When one doll broke her leg, a wee wheelchair was created. When Marvin Douglas wants a fresh supply of building material to make, perhaps for a child's rocking horse, he goes down to the local mill and gathers up scrap headed for the incinerator. He shapes. He smoothes. He glues. He lacquers. And there's a poplar steed for riding! He cuts. He welds. He climbs. He builds an iron windmill for no other reason than to watch the vanes turned by the winds of Grove Ridge Road.

He gathers the stone. He fits. He levels. He cements. And there's his combination incinerator/outdoor grill. (It takes a mean piece of wood for Marvin Douglas to burn it.) He's an electrician. He's a plumber. "I do it all. I don't have to hire anything done," says Marvin to his visitor, who is green with envy.

"What are the traits of a good carpenter, Mr. Douglas?"

"Able to work hard. Confidence. Ability to try to do good. Always looking for new ideas."

And to Jane: "What are the basics in business that you've taught your students these past thirty-eight years?"

"Be honest. Have integrity."

*David*

# WAITING FOR THE WINTER, LOVING THE LOVELY

oventry Kersey Dighton Patmore, the nineteenth-century English poet, wrote warmly for twentieth- and twenty-first century Kentuckians:

"I, singularly moved to love the lovely that are not beloved, of all the seasons, most Love Winter."

The fashion for many (Eskimos not counted) is to loathe rather that to love winter. To lovers in Camelot, this seems out of joint. "Eternal Spring," as it's accurately proclaimed in Venezuela and many other tropical "paradises," is as boring as it is beautiful, as bland as it is bountiful.

Not to experience the beauty and the loveliness of winter is to miss the miracle of the snowflakes, individually marvelous, unique as fingerprints, unrepeatable as spider webs.

In 1988, Thanksgiving came and went without snow to decorate our windows. There was no sledding back and forth across the hill to Grandmother or Grandfather's house, no foretaste of better snows to come. There was neither skiff nor whiff of one. Weren't there snows once upon a time at Thanksgiving? Perhaps it was only a dream. Maybe I only read about it in fairy tales.

"I'm Dreaming of a White Christmas" was a song calculated to put a lump in any normal throat. I suppose that's history, along with "Rudolph the Red-Nosed Reindeer" and "Up on the Rooftop." There was a time when Christmas without snow was a rare disappointment. Now there's a collective sigh of relief when "Old Person Winter" has better things to do, better places to visit.

A Christmas Eve snowfall about midnight is as lovely a sight as any I could imagine. Yet we walked about this December 25th as if brown were the appropriate and expected color. If there'd been a snowstorm, for heaven's sake, there would have been dire warnings about impending head-on collisions on interstate highways. The wind-chill factor has become the national discomfort index, and many moan and groan accordingly.

My heart of hearts cries out for the one-horse sleigh. While Lalie and I bided our time in Venezuela's "Eternal Spring," I fantasized a brisk romp down the Plum Lick Road, Old Dobbin's mane flying, nostrils flaring, steam jetting like popped-off boilers. Lovers would be warm beneath a great wool blanket, and their child would nestle between them, storing enough memories to last another sixty winters.

There is neither old nor new Dobbin. There is no sleigh. There is no great wool blanket. Plum Lick Road has been dry. Old Person Winter has whistled a few times from the top to the bottom of the stone chimney of the big house, and Chief, the rottweiller, has been brought in to spend the night on the back porch. Ewedawg has huddled in the vicinity of the sheep. The cattle have bunched together by the rolls of hay on the edge of Plum Lick Creek. But the woodpile behind the meat house is about as tall as it was last winter and the winter before. The whole notion of winter as an identifiable season has been strangely postponed from Thanksgiving to Christmas to New Year's to the beginning of Lent.

I hope that sixty winters have taught me that Mother Nature and Winter, her child, march to different drummers than I. I have no choice but to comply. They do not wait on me, but I on them. I must pick up my drum and walk in step with the natural world. Artificiality may be comforting, but I cannot rejoice that winter has so far not reduced my woodpile.

The problem, I think, is that one hundred years after Coventry Kersey Dighton Patmore, my generation is more concerned with comfort than with loveliness, more fascinated with unimpeded speed than with the slower crunch of hooves in new fallen snow. Some even prefer electronically generated graphics over finger tracings on frosted windowpanes.

Perhaps, says I, I'll spend some small part of the ten of my three score and ten sitting in the several rocking chairs of this old house, and I'll more patiently wait for the changing of the seasons' guards. If winter be late, then winter be late. If spring be delayed, then spring be delayed.

I rest my case.

*David*

# PART THREE

*A fundamental question is whether we desire to keep our feet firmly planted in the nineteenth or earlier centuries, or if we long to discover the new worlds of the twenty-first or later centuries.*

*"The principle of modesty is the governing principle," he says, his manner exemplifying the thought, his narrow suspenders a symbol of a different attitude about how one should live.*

# GET A GOOD EDUCATION, SON

*T*he stepfather and the son were bouncing along in an old pickup truck. Nip, the bird dog, sat between them. His brown eyes were fixed upon the road ahead, loyalty being his comfort.

Truth lived in unstructured windows of time.

There was a coming coolness of early autumn in the air, an unpredictable but welcomed refreshment. There were thoughts of woodcutting and the pleasure that comes with the first building of a friendly fire. It included the warming of hands extended to the kitchen stove.

After more than fifty years, the clarity of the remembrance has not dimmed.

"Get a good education, Son."

Nip and the boy heard the somber voice. When it spoke, they listened. They came by this attentiveness naturally. They shared trust, respect, and doing intuitively the right thing. Children, not yet entertained with televised violence, felt the coolness of their mornings. "Get a good education" was a message appreciated for its possibilities.

"It's something nobody can take away from you," the father quietly concluded.

The thrust of the unhurried, nonthreatening remark blew into an impressionable corner of the young boy's developing mind. There was no specific or urgent direction.

The driver of the pickup truck might have said more. He might have scolded and breathed fire and spoken direly of unemployment and frustrated talent. But he didn't. He might have spoken of fine automobiles and long driveways to million-dollar mansions. But he didn't. He didn't speak of the latest technology, but he left open the door to many possibilities.

Autumns rolled by with metronomic ease. The old man went to his reward. Nip went to his. The boy grew toward adulthood.

There were the Ivy League and the Big Ten schools and plenty of exclusive places to get that "good education," but loyalty pointed the way to a liberal arts education at the University of Kentucky. Heading in that direction was as natural as Old Nip knowing a good thing when he saw it. It was a best-kept secret.

Donovan Hall was a recently completed dormitory for men in 1948. Could it have been almost fifty years ago? We thought we were mighty fortunate, and we were.

There were professors like Niel Plummer, who taught Introduction to Journalism and Etymology, and William Ward, who taught Romantic Poetry, and Ben Black, who taught Shakespeare, and Wally Briggs and Lolo Robinson, who taught theater arts. There were so many more fine teachers. All of them gave far more than they ever got.

Hollis Summers, who taught creative writing, required his students to bring a fresh idea to each meeting of the class. Imagine that! He also advised us to throw away the first page of everything we wrote.

William Jansen taught folklore. He was a nationally and internationally acclaimed scholar who also appreciated the value of "the dirty joke."

Herman Spivey caused Dreiser, Crane, Norris, and Twain to seem fundamental to seeing the American phenomenon through the translucence of fine literature. Dr. Spivey made Ralph Waldo Emerson, Walt Whitman and Henry David Thoreau understandable and needed.

A student who memorized answers to literary and philosophical theories could not fool Thomas Stroup. "You have obviously memorized this but do you understand it?"

Hill Shine did what he could to make the Victorian poets feel at home in a pickup truck mentality, but it was not to be. As they say, some things, like good wine, take a little longer. Perhaps Dr. Shine understood that "a good education" comes too early for some. Given time it has a better chance to flower.

J. LARKINS

Some of the youth who rode in Kentucky pickup trucks never had that chance. They went off to World War II, and they didn't come back. The next time you're in Memorial Coliseum for "Midnight Madness" or on graduation day in the spring of another year, take a few moments to look at the names on the walls leading to the upper level. You may be astounded when you realize how many of our best and brightest never came back. They made it possible for the living to have a better chance for "the good education." They should not be forgotten.

After more than twenty-five years working as a professional journalist, I reminded myself not to forget my alma mater. I came back to teach for more than ten years before "retiring" again.

Now I'm back in my own pickup truck, a dog named Pumpkin by my side. There's another beginning, the best part of my life. My goal is to write about Kentucky for Kentuckians.

There's no doubt in my mind that the successful outcome has been built on the "good education" that I received at the University of Kentucky.

*David*

# DR. CLARK

*W*hen I think of Kentucky and living in it quietly and thoughtfully, I think of one man–Thomas D. Clark.

When I think of the quintessence of Kentuckians, the voice of the land pioneered by Boone, Walker, and Gist, the place more than 3.6 million individuals today call home, I think of Thomas Dionysius Clark, the historian emeritus of the Commonwealth of Kentucky.

His middle name alone has a rich history. Dionysius Exiguus is considered to be "one of the most learned men" of the sixth century. Dionysius of Alexandria "showed wisdom and moderation in the controversies" of the third century. Dionysius of Halicarnassus wrote a history of Rome down to 264 B.C., and Dionysius the Elder "was a poet and patron of poets and philosophers" in the first century B.C. (Cambridge University Press is the source for these acclaims in its *Chambers Biographical Dictionary*.)

Kentucky's twentieth-century Dionysius, in his 95th year, was born in Louisville, Mississippi (they pronounce it LEWIS-ville), July 14, 1903.

Recently, when attending the funeral service for 105-year-old George Fugate, a quiet Kentuckian, native of Letcher County, I had the honor of signing the visitor's register just under the name of Thomas D. Clark. It was at that moment that I knew I'd write this tribute to him, an example of bringing flowers to the living.

My wife gave me a wonderful Christmas present this past year. I have it beside me now. It's a rare first-edition copy of Dr. Tom Clark's *The Kentucky*, personally inscribed at last year's Kentucky Book Fair. The book, one of *The Rivers of America* series, includes the soul-stirring woodcut illustrations of John A. Spelman III. Stephen Vincent Benèt and Carl Carmer edited the series. The retail price of the book, when it was first published in 1942, was $2.50.

Chapter One takes the reader to the headwaters of the Kentucky River: "The Kentucky is not alone a river or a drainage system, it is a way of life." Chapter Two recounts the amazing tale of John Swift's Silver: " 'Boys, don't never quit hunting fer it. It is the richest thing I ever saw. It will make Kentucky rich.' "

What will make Kentucky rich will be the discovery, the rediscovery, and the preservation of the memory of one Thomas Dionysius Clark. After all, who among us has written more prodigiously? *The Beginning of the L&N; A History of Kentucky* (the copy on my shelf is the sixth edition); *The Rampaging Frontier; Pills, Petticoats and Plows; The Rural Press and the New South; The Southern Country Editor; Pleasant Hill in the Civil War;* and *Agrarian Kentucky.*

Dr. Tom Clark was responsible for leading in the creation of the Special Collections section of the University of Kentucky Library and of the University Press of Kentucky. His life as a teacher is legendary (University of Kentucky, Eastern Kentucky University, Indiana University, Harvard, Chicago, Stanford, and many other institutions of higher learning). I shall not be soon forgetting the year I invited him to teach a course in history of journalism at the University of Kentucky. I was dismayed that there were a number of complaints, especially the one that said, "He didn't give multiple choice tests, he just stood up there and talked."

The last time I saw Dr. Clark, the weight of ninety-five years of living and writing and suffering insufferable students kindly was bending him over. But never mind that. When we came to a door, he graciously stood back to allow me to go first.

The final chapter of Dr. Thomas D. Clark's *The Kentucky* is titled: "This is the Kentucky." On page 402, there is this: "The Kentucky River country is not altogether a land of colonels and the frivolous things which have been advertised as Kentucky. Really, underneath all the glamorous surface both in the mountains and in the Bluegrass, there are thousands of plain everyday people who go about their daily affairs making an honest living and enjoying the lives they live."

*David*

132

# MISSISSIPPI WOMAN, KENTUCKY GRANDMOTHER

━━━━━━━━━━━━━━━ ✥ ━━━━━━━━━━━━━━━

*A*s the sun sets over Lake Mary–a lovely, lonesome moon-shaped body of water deserted by the meandering main channel of the Mississippi River– a southern lady reminisces in the cool of the evening, recalling her Kentucky roots.

"My grandmother was Leona Pace Morgan," says Polly Rosenblatt, who now makes her home south of Natchez, where I grew up and where I return as often as possible to be with another southern lady, my mother, who also has roots in Kentucky. We all love to sit and play catch-up. It's rare that the conversation turns back upriver to Kentucky in quite the way it did out there on Lake Mary this summer. Out there, the mosquitoes will walk off with you if you're not careful and you'll also want to watch out for real wildcats, not the stuffed or costumed kind.

"Grandmother was a surgical nurse for the Frontier Nursing Service in Leslie county," Polly explains with pride about her mother's mother. Polly was only three years old when she and her parents left the mountains of Eastern Kentucky. They moved over to Pewee Valley near Louisville, and now Polly has a family of her own, deep in the farthest southwestern corner of Mississippi. She likes to share with her children some of the lessons she learned from Grandmother Leona in the same way my daughter has learned about her family through her grandmother, Eulalie (the origin of "Lalie," the first name by which I'm most often called).

"There was a time when she'd never seen a light bulb," said Polly of Leona. "The first time, she said she stood there turning it on and off about a hundred times."

After working her way through nursing school in Pennsylvania (earning money by knitting sweaters), the young, enthusiastic Leona received a letter from Mary Breckinridge, founder in 1925 of what would become the

Frontier Nursing Service. It was a personal invitation for Leona to return to her native Kentucky to help the people of Leslie County.

With darkness settling over the giant river I love so much, the Mississippi, fed by every drop of Kentucky waters, my friend Polly recalls the days when she'd return in summers to visit with her grandmother back home in the mountains of Eastern Kentucky. Polly and Leona would spend precious time together, fishing, talking, connecting the years.

"She loved to fish. She was a living example of a person who decided to do something and then did it. Most strong-willed. A doer. Make things happen. Mover and shaker. Overcame hardships she had growing up."

Polly dug down deep: "I was quite young. It was almost dark. She had a pickup truck. We drove as far as we could go and then got out and walked. We had to walk a long way straight up where rocks were coming out of the ground. It was slippery. The front porch was at least twenty feet off the ground with dog and chickens underneath and the back of the house into the mountain. There was a smell like old pork fat cooking."

"To make lard?"

"Yes, maybe so. I remember that there was somebody she knew. When they saw her coming, a man came down off the porch and held her hand while she went up the rickety steps. Mountain men didn't usually do that. She told me before she got there that I would have to sit on the porch. A lady was sick. Grandmother was living out Isaiah, 49:11: 'He shall feed his flock like a shepherd; he shall gather the lambs with his arms, and carry them in his bosom, and shall gently lead those that are with young.'

"Seemed like a long time. Got dark. They were sitting on the porch peeling apples for apple butter. They didn't talk. They peeled hundreds of apples–many bushels. They were using a kerosene lamp. Somebody was in the kitchen cooking apples."

134

Leona didn't tell her granddaughter what had happened at the sickbed. Maybe Leona felt it wouldn't be right to tell everything.

By now, the darkness over Lake Mary had drooped down like a shroud where the Homochitto River empties the waters from the east.

Polly recalled another time: "I was not allowed out of the truck. We went through a creek bed. Had a gallon of buttermilk for somebody and I had to balance it while going over the creek bed. A man was going to die. People in the mountains had uncanny knowledge of when people were going to die. When the coffeepot was set out, in twenty-four hours somebody would die. There'd be a wake."

"People would come and prepare the body?"

"Yes. The wake sometimes went on for days."

Polly remembered Christmas with Leona: "She'd take country hams to people who lived at the head of the hollow. She viewed the Frontier Nursing Service as one of the best health organizations that could have come into the eastern Kentucky mountains–people truly having a mission to help others."

For Polly and me it has been a delightful evening for building memory bridges. We share in our connection with home sweet Kentucky.

Night closes around Lake Mary where the Mississippi River echoes with the sounds of the bayou creatures signaling the time for southern ladies to turn toward home.

*Lalie*

# LOUISE

"*H*oney, I should be at home in bed now," said the eighty-two-year-old lady doctor after she'd bounded down the hallway of her office on Main Street in Morehead. Dressed in white, a stethoscope hanging from her neck, she had thrust out her hand, the firm grip not nearly what I had expected.

Named national "Country Doctor of the Year" for 1994-1995, Claire Louise Caudill may be short of stature, and her frequent smiles just might be mistaken. Back in the old days she was delivering babies deep in the highlands of Rowan County. If an anxious father rushed in where he didn't belong, the lady who'd traveled many a hard mile to bring new life into the world might have had to backhand the gentleman entirely out of the way. "When he grabbed for the head of the baby, I got rid of him right quick."

Dr. Caudill, also honored this year by the Women's Center of Central Kentucky (an organization whose mission it is to help women develop skills), flexed her left arm muscles and laughed one of her deep laughs. "I've always been strong," she added.

"What's a typical day at present?" I asked.

"Today, I went to the hospital about 8:30, picked up papers, lab reports, saw patients, came to the office."

Dr. Caudill keeps nine-to-four office hours Monday, Tuesday, Thursday, and Friday. "Saturday is a no–go."

"How many patients do you see a day?"

"Around twenty. It's variable. Don't deliver babies now. Haven't for eleven years. I've changed my practice from obstetrics to geriatrics!" Dr. Caudill laughed, the richness of it seeming to start in her toes then moving upward toward her hands and finally to her eyes.

"A girl came in. Wanted to know if she was pregnant. She was. She had wanted birth control pills. I always try to talk to them a little bit."

C. Louise Caudill wanted to be a doctor ever since she was "a little kid." She received degrees from Ohio State University, Columbia University in New York, the University of Louisville, the University of Kentucky, and Thomas More College. She's taught at Morehead State University and the University of Kentucky. She's a member of the American Academy of Family Physicians.

Louise met her associate, Susie Halbleib, at Oneida near Manchester in Clay County. Susie was from Louisville, but she and Louise are committed to Rowan County. Louise, the doctor, and Susie, the nurse, practice medicine on Main Street in Morehead, where patients come in for such routine matters as "removal of heavy ear wax."

The two pioneer women have traveled up and down the hollows of eastern Kentucky. "Every way except by helicopter...all over Rowan, Elliott and Menifee Counties...sometimes by boat to see a patient...We'd leave our car, and they'd come for us...We'd be picked up in wagon or sleigh.

"One woman thought she had pneumonia, but she was going to have a baby. The roads were creek beds...roads were terrible...Patients paid us or didn't...We didn't trade. We went to deliver a baby where the family had just had dinner. There were chickens on the table, pigs underneath.

"I delivered the first baby on February 2, 1934–and I walked a long distance."

"How many babies have you delivered?"

"About 8,000...have no idea, really. Lots of twins, but no triplets!"

"How old were the mothers?"

"From thirteen to forty-seven," said Susie as she walked by.

"Dr. Caudill, to what do you credit your long life?"

"Made out of good stuff!" she answered. "My grandmother was a big woman...made her own medicine...roots and bark."

"Any plans for retirement?"

"I've retired several times...most every day...but for some reason I wind up here every morning. I don't know what I'm going to do. I guess when I can't get here, I'll quit. When you don't have a reason to get up, you die...so...be happy and enjoy what you do."

"Don't worry?"

"Worry can drive you crazy if you aren't already there! Eat right and exercise. I played tennis up until three years ago. Now I swim twenty minutes a day."

"Hobbies?"

"Reading mysteries, fiction, biographies. Travel. Never had high ideals. Wanted to be right here as a doctor."

"How did you deal with a male-dominated profession?"

"Men dominate instead of cooperate. They own instead of share. They are taught that. One of the best ways to get along is to believe men are superior, and we women have to take care of that. We have to be kind, sweet, sophisticated, and smooth. Those are the words today; could be different tomorrow."

"What advice do you have for young girls?"

"Listen to your mother."

"What advice do you have for young people who want to be doctors?"

"Do the routine things to get to medical school."

"How do you feel about a national medical program?"

"We need some kind of general health care. Don't know, but the best care comes locally. We were built on democracy."

Dr. C. Louise Caudill and nurse Susan Halbleib are among the strongest and the wisest of Kentucky women, and they just might be role models for what ails us.

Today, St. Claire Medical Center, founded by Dr. Caudill in 1962, serves its many patients as a regional hospital–and the memory of this good woman lives on after her death, New Year's Eve, 1998.

*Lalie*

# MOTHER'S LESSONS

$\mathcal{T}$here were three main things my best friend, my mother, always told me. Maybe yours told you something along these same lines:

Stand on your own two feet, go out into the world and try it on for size, and always remember to show respect for your elders. I did that. It was scary at times. I took some pretty hard falls, but I always remembered the part about "stand on your own two feet," and I managed to pull myself up again. Maybe I wouldn't have had the courage if the other "Eulalie" (my mother and I have the same name) had not kept pushing me out the door and telling me that I had to do my own thing in my own way in my own time. "Think for yourself," she'd admonish.

My world included trying lots of things. I was a little theatre dancer and an oil field technician. I was a secretary and a draftsman (I prefer that word to "draftswoman" or "draftsperson"), an auto mechanic and a social worker. There were all those long flights back and forth from New York to Buenos Aires and Philadelphia to San Francisco when I worked for an international cosmetics company. There was plenty of turbulence and I acquired some learning bruises along the way, but I slathered the lumps and bumps with the salve of my Louisiana/Mississippi mother's encouragement and kept on going.

Yes, I always remembered what mother said about "respect your elders," and I was never ashamed about saying "Yes, Ma'am" and "No, Sir" and "Please may I..." (New York's Madison Avenue mavens ate it up like candy and begged for more.)

Well, after I came in off the road and settled down with my husband, my newest best friend, my mentor, and the man I want only to please, along comes this little girl, my little girl. Life has a way of coming full circle. So here goes:

Dear Daughter (she's twelve, going on twenty-two):

"Stand on your own two feet, go out into the world and try it on for size, and always remember to respect your elders.

"When you fall and bruise yourself, I won't be there to pick you up and powder your nose. Of course, if I were there I'd be Johnnie on the spot. In reality, I'd lay down my life for you. But you wouldn't want it that way. You'd naturally want to do your own thing in your own way in your own time.

"You might want to be an astronaut. Or a deep-sea diver. Didn't you tell me the other day you wanted to be a marine biologist? Well, you go for it. And it all begins right now in the seventh grade. It starts with caring passionately about the truth. I know, there are those times of temptation when it seems easier to paper over the truth and, frankly, there are those special times when telling the lonesome truth can hurt more than it can help. But 99.9 percent of the time you'll do better when you're honest with others. Of course, you can't be honest with anybody if you don't begin by being honest with yourself.

"Peer pressure? It's real. I know it is. I felt it when I was twelve and sixteen and twenty-one and all the way up the line to right now. But you know what I think you should do? I think you should look all those peer buddies right in the eye and tell 'em, you all can go and do the wrong thing if you want to, but I'm going to try my best to do the right thing, because that's what my mama told me.

"No matter what happens, you just remember one big thing: I love you. And so does your daddy."

Well, this was something I just felt like saying, now that I'm moving into my second half-century. And maybe my telling it in this way has something to do with the fact that recently I went back on the road again. Only this time I went to be with my mother while she was in the hospital. We spent three weeks of quality time together. We looked into each other's eyes, we two Eulalies did, and what we saw we wouldn't trade for anything out there in the bright and shining twenty-first century world. We saw trust. We felt love. And we came out of that hospital together and went to her home to see about making her as comfortable and peaceful as possible for as long as she lives.

We're both still standing on our own two feet. We're not traveling as much as we used to. But one thing is for certain: we've got more respect for each other than we've ever had before in our lives. And that feeling is warm and honest and good.

Epilogue:

I wish my parents had lived to see this book dedicated to them. Eulalie passed away, quietly, early on Good Friday morning, April 2, 1999. To age eighty-eight, she lived a full, productive, and courageous quarter of a century longer than did my father, Charles, who died at age fifty-seven in 1973. They are still on call and mentoring me on a daily basis, urging me to be the best at whatever the task at hand.

*Lalie*

# HANDS ON THE HUMANITIES

*A* good liberal arts education for a preacher, politician, businessperson, journalist, or tiller of the soil is as elemental as oxygen, without which their lungs would wither and die. The hue and cry for "hands-on experience" in higher education is a contradiction in terms at best. The immediate question becomes: "Hands on what?" "Why?" and "To what effect?"

It's one thing to know how to push buttons. A far better consideration is to know why to push them at all. When a whole culture is reduced to a rabble of robots, "human beings" go home on weekends to do whatever they want. A weekend of pleasure is of little value if a five-day period has been mortgaged to make the purchase.

A good liberal arts education should include a deep appreciation of the humanities. Classical literature is a starting point, but it is too often lost in a dead sea of pop culture in which too many of us are thrashing or sometimes treading water to keep from drowning. English and American literature are fertile fields for the study of the humanities, areas so rich as to invigorate and validate our own experiences in these last days of the twentieth century.

We should generalize in order to specialize, then return to the general to authenticate the special. What's needed is simply to see the bigger picture, to be able to see the forest despite the trees. A good liberal arts education includes an incentive to take a few steps back from favorite preoccupations, usual habits, and stubborn inclinations to consider afresh the possibilities arising from native intelligence. The tragedy is that many of us waste an entire lifetime doing exactly what we weren't meant to do in the first place. Instead of working on an assembly line to produce planned obsolescence (automobiles or neckties), some of us might be discovering new Robert Penn Warren poetry or John Jacob Niles music. There's also the possibility that more of us might be making important contributions to the cause of global peace and the reduction of human suffering.

There's time to do the things we really want to do and really need to do. True wealth is the accomplishment of true humanitarianism, not the mindless accumulation of money. Capital gain is the motor that drives the national engine, and money makes the Commonwealth purr down the toll roads and interstate highways. There's nothing in my argument to minimize the importance of industrial development. But if all we do is drive and purr, then we've missed something vital to the natural genius. Call it soul. Call it character. Call it decency. No matter what we choose to call it, it is the better part of our natural selves. It is the loving part.

A good liberal arts education will sustain us well beyond the ivory towers of academe. It will save us in the end from bitterness borne of living mechanistic, monetarily measured existences. Kentuckians can be proud after running their courses. They can stand on the banks of the Ohio, Big Sandy, Cumberland, Tennessee, Green, Barren, Salt, Licking, and Kentucky rivers, and they can testify to the other forty-nine states that they have cared about the truest education of people, especially themselves.

We begin with the children. We start with the babies we conceive and very soon hold in our arms. We sacrifice more than we thought possible to insure that these smallest of miracles will have the fullest opportunities to develop their compassion as well as their minds and certainly as well as their hands. At our greatest peril do we desert them to a popular culture of bells, whistles, and thingamabobs.

We can't help the children until we help ourselves–another contradiction of terms. "Hands-on experience" of whatever kind will never substitute for the liberal arts education carefully and lovingly considered. One of the best hands-on experiences can be reaching for the off knob on the television set and extending the arm and hand for the book on the shelf. There's hardly any thoughtful television journalist I know who does not advocate less rather than more total television viewing time in the area of knowledge gathering. Walter Cronkite, Eric Sevareid, and Dan Rather are three I personally have known who agree that too many are receiving too much of their "news" from television at the expense of books, periodicals, newspapers, and radio.

Variety and differences in point of view are key aspects of the good liberal arts education. It is also well for Westerners to remember that there is an Eastern civilization. Cross-cultural education has become increasingly necessary and rewarding for anyone striving for a better grasp of the humanities on a global scale at a time when Earth is becoming smaller and smaller. Hands-on experience and a good liberal arts education need not be mutually exclusive. The goal is to bring them together in greater compatibility. The day may come when the hand that is on the plow will be in direct connection with the eye that is on the sparrow and the mind that is on all mankind.

*David*

# LESLIE

$L$eslie Kendrick of Paintsville has picked up her academic and natural skills like a nine-pound hammer and has smashed every stereotype ever written about Eastern Kentucky.

She has won a Rhodes Scholarship at age twenty-one.

Leslie's mother, Leatha, is a teacher. Leslie's father, Will, is an attorney. Two younger daughters, Eliza and Lyda, are coming on strong and well in a tightly knit Farm Bureau family of achievers. They are anchored to a farm in the East Point section of Johnson County, but their outreach cuts across county, state, and national boundaries.

To speak with Leslie by telephone in her room at the University of North Carolina, where she's in her second year, is to hear a clear and kind Appalachian voice. To break bread with her parents, Leatha and Will, near the head of the Bert T. Combs Mountain Parkway is to understand the stuff in which Rhodes Scholars are sometimes fortunate enough to be rooted.

To say the family is "anchored" to the farm is not to say that it's in any way potbound. Being a Farm Bureau family does not mean an inevitability of tangled, decaying roots, nor the basis for a "Kentucky Cycle." With the support and encouragement of her parents, Leslie decided at age twelve to be tested by Duke University. A very high score (top 2 percent) and a Hugh O'Brien Leadership Conference later led to Leslie's independent decision to enroll for her last two years of high school in the Salem Academy in Winston Salem, North Carolina.

"Summer traveling in Europe, Oxford for a day, a program in classics and English, studying after graduation" resulted in the next step, the University of North Carolina, where Leslie Kendrick of Johnson County, Kentucky, writes papers in Latin. Her heroes? "My mom and my dad and Samuel Johnson," says Leslie. "You know he wrote a dictionary."

Leslie's field of study, classics and English, reaches for the stars, but she has not forsaken her Eastern Kentucky heritage. She, like Dr. Johnson, is "haunted by the parable of the talents, the importance of utilizing gifts, using gifts to the finest."

In the preface to his *Dictionary of the English Language*, Samuel Johnson wrote, "Where there are many things to be done, each must be allowed its share of time and labor, in the proportion only which it bears to the whole; nor can it be expected that the stones which form the dome of a temple should be squared and polished like the diamond of a ring."

In this context, Leslie Kendrick believes that gifted children should not be left alone to the possibilities of their genius. "You can't expect [gifted] children to fulfill all their talents on their own. They need support. They should not be denied the opportunity to excel," Leslie explains.

Leslie Kendrick's achievement is the result of caring parents who read to her in her childhood. Her adulthood was built on a foundation of books. She did not succumb to television. She did not cave in to peer pressure. Leslie thrived on "personal preference and initiative."

With tears in her eyes, her mother recalls, "I fell in love with her the moment she was born. She has been an inspiration to me. She has a sweetness about her that her sisters share."

Leslie says she has "encountered some sort of stereotyping of Appalachia, a concept of what Appalachia is." She calls the talk "inaccurate and uninformed. It [Appalachia] is nowhere as isolated as it used to be. The Mountain Parkway is two hours to Lexington." Coincidentally, this yellow brick road is two hours from Lexington to Paintsville-Prestonsburg. The "way out" is also a "way in."

"I don't know where I'm going," says Leslie as she prepares for her years of study at Oxford University in England. She wants to be an English professor like her mother who this spring will make the four-hour roundtrip to Lexington to teach at the University of Kentucky.

In the words of her mother as she prepares for the day her daughter will depart the hills: "The gift will be returned in ways I can't speculate. We are sending a gift. Eastern Kentucky is sending a gift to the rest of the world."

*Lalie*

146

# MOON OVER MIAMI

*I*'m writing from a motel room in Miami (1991). I did not want to be here.

Even if I could afford one of the yachts on Biscayne Bay, as a matter of choice I wouldn't want to be here. I'd rather walk on a farm in home sweet Kentucky than sail on a yacht on the edge of Miami.

I thought it was important for me to learn more about journalism education, so I flew down here for a meeting of the Secondary Education Division of the Association for Education Journalism and Mass Communication. I was up at four a.m. to begin thinking about the day ahead at the *Miami Herald*, sponsor of a daylong seminar on writing, copy editing, graphic design, and newspaper composition. One of the best parts of the seminar was called "adopt a pro." I selected a community columnist.

Robert L. Steinback was my pro: a tall, lanky, outgoing African-American. His column appeared twice a week in the *Miami Herald*. He didn't have the luxury of writing about sheep. He was writing about people. While I was there, Cuban-Americans had accused an African-American minister on the public payroll as an ethnic mediator of making anti-Hispanic remarks. The minister vowed to appeal his suspension.

Robert Steinback was under deadline pressure to try to make sense out of the controversy. He told me how easy it would be to push any or all of the emotional buttons. With one column he could become the hero of the African-American community or the savior of the Hispanic leadership or the villain for both. Steinback believed his column should argue a case built upon fact and reason. He resisted the temptation to tell people only what he believed they wanted to hear. Mr. Steinback didn't care if people–African-American, Hispanic, or Caucasian–didn't "like" him. What mattered most was whether the column made people think or, better yet, caused them to rethink their positions.

"Don't blacks accuse you of working for a white-dominated management, making you unable to represent black interests?" I asked.

"Yes, they do."

"What do you say to them?"

"I say, I don't want to represent a black point of view, or any point of view. Management doesn't tell me what to write, or what not to write. If they ever did, I would stop writing the column. All I have is my credibility."

When I arrived back on Plum Lick, I said to myself, credibility doesn't mean money. It means trust and believability. Miami can keep all its yachts. Give me the courage and insight to write better. That's the best way to sail off into sunsets.

*David*

# NAME-CALLING

In the name of better race relations, "black" became "people of color" and then "African-American." Since neither blacks nor people of color are in agreement, the choice is a matter better left to individual discretion. There was a time when Negro was preferred and "black" was considered a racial slur. "Black" became "beautiful" and "Negro" fell by the wayside. Before "Negro" there was "negro" and before that there was the word that got changed in "My Old Kentucky Home." All along there's been a most racially offensive epithet. Using this word has been a little like yelling "peckerwood" in a crowded Pikeville theater.

The piece of work at hand is to try to make a case for calling people what they are: people.

For the most part, Kentucky has come a long way in this regard; its track record is considerably better than that of states to the south or north. The Commonwealth has a long tradition of fairness, the American Indian being a tragic exception.

The downside to name-calling and social labeling is the hurt. It drives otherwise good people farther apart. As a youth from the Bluegrass, I spent summers in Cincinnati and was sneered at by faster talking big city kids. That name-calling was as bad as bumblebee stings on top of the head.

"Peckerwood" was highly offensive, and "silly billy," "hick," and "country bumpkin" were fighting words. Being called a "Little Abner" or "Moonbeam McSwine" was not calculated to make any Kentuckian's day. The name-calling didn't end there. Anybody caught spending too much time with books became a "bookworm." Soon a gauntlet was thrown down and on either side stood the "boneheads," "fatheads," "meatheads," "mushheads," "know-nothings," "nitwits," and "nincompoops." With their long two-by-fours they whipped up on the defenseless "smart alecks," "eggheads," and "educated idiots/fools."

This was the theme played to the hilt by Presidential Peckerwood George Corley Wallace, who dismissed most college teachers as "pointy-headed professors who don't know how to park their bicycles straight." The governor also said that if you made them open up their briefcases all you'd probably find inside would be "a peanut butter sandwich."

There's a whole category of class-conscious epithets including "aristocrats," "bluebloods," "mama's darlings," "silk stockings," "yuppies," and "wimps." On the opposite end of the mudslinging might be found "crumb bums," "longhairs," "hippies," "dopeheads," "winos," "bag ladies," "hobos," "Joads," "rednecks," "cedar choppers," "grubbers," "moochers," "spongers," and "happy pappies."

In the miscellaneous category there are the "nervous Nellies," "eager beavers," and "peeping Toms."

The underlying idea for most of these weapons is to insult and thereby demean the other person in order to enhance the speaker's supposed feeling of superiority. What's the matter, can't they take a joke? The best jokes from the joker's point of view are usually at the expense of the joked about. It involves pointing a ridiculing finger at a perceived weakness. The more grotesque the effect, the better the outcome.

Language doesn't matter. The old proverb of "sticks and stones may break my bones, but words can never harm me" is in serious need of new consideration. A word often is as devastating as an arrow, and the careless use of a phonetic phenomenon can be just as piercing. It's tiresome to be characterized meanly or stereotyped in any way, the more so if it's done with vengeance. Universal peace depends on a commonwealth of thoughtful consideration for all the people all the time. A thoughtless word sent out from the quiver of accumulated insensitivity or rank meanspiritness is a shame.

The better way is to stop the name-calling and labeling altogether. People are people no matter their color or their station in life at any particular moment. Some need help. Most need respect. All need love.

*David*

150

# MAMA

*M*ost called her Mama.

She had a special right to the title, even though she had no natural children of her own.

She was Mama because she taught school for fifty-four years.

She was Mama because over the years she took all kinds of children, black and white, into her heart.

And maybe Miss Minerva was Mama because at 110 years of age this beautiful, calm, dignified woman was a role model for the present and the future.

"Advice for students? Mind their parents. Don't lay in the streets. Nothing there for you. Keep [your] hand in God's hand. God knows all the children. My mother was a pillar in the church. I had a good mother and father. I became an organist in the church."

Advice for parents and teachers of children? "Be firm with them. Don't give in. Honey, I'm telling you, bring them up in prayer. Bring them up in church. Pray and go to church."

At 110, Mama sat quietly in her wheelchair on the second floor of Bourbon Heights in Paris, Kentucky. There was a small table in front of Mama's lap. It was loaded with cards, letters, and pictures from students and friends across the nation.

"I raised so many in my home. I was retired about three years when they integrated the schools...had the first grade for thirty years, then the third grade, then the fifth grade...There are people who are now eighty years old and I taught them their ABC's."

Policemen wrote her cards. Former servicemen remembered Mama and took the time to write to her. Former students and foster children sent pictures. Mama threw nothing away.

"I save everything," said Mama, whose mother's father was a slave. "He was the best carpenter in the county."

Anger hardly simmered, if at all, in Mama. But she remembered. She hadn't forgotten how much less she was paid than white teachers. "They didn't pay us chicken feed," said Mama with the softest of smiles. A picture on her table showed her standing tall by the side of rows of black children. When I went by to visit with her in 1996, though, Mama couldn't stand. She didn't say, "They amputated my legs" or "They removed my legs," or "I lost my legs" (to diabetes)–she said, with her honest and direct manner, "They cut them off."

Still, Mama didn't bemoan the fact that she no longer had legs upon which to stand. There was the beautiful face, the neatly combed hair (that once was down to her waist), with the perfectly tied ribbon, and the warm grasp of her hands.

"I lived in the good days. Now they make laws that children don't have to be punished. You can't expect them to do anything."

Even when Mama said, "I don't have strength to do anything," she smiled, and it was a way of making visitors feel grateful for all they still possess. She was often asked the question, "How do you account for the fact that you've lived to be 110?"

Her reply: "When I was young I ate a lot of onions, which helped to keep me well...I lived by the side of the road to be a friend to man...I loved my mother and father."

"Never married?"

"Men are treacherous...don't want to be bothered with no man!"

Mama did enjoy watching men's wrestling on television. She didn't say why she enjoyed it so much. Maybe it was because it was a lesson, a show and tell, seeing treachery trying to outdo itself.

Mama stayed home. She took in washing and ironing. "I helped soldiers, Indians, Africans...[I tried to] stand high in the community."

"Did you ever smoke or drink?"

"No, ma'am," she replied with laughter. "My daddy didn't drink. He was a hard-working man."

"What's the future, Mama?"

"I've got my ticket, and I'm on my way to Heaven."

A nurse entered the room. She walked up to the lady in the wheelchair. The young nurse spoke:

"Are you ready for lunch, Mama?"

Mama said she was. And the last time I saw her was when the elevator door closed. But I didn't intend for it to be the last time I saw Miss Minerva Bedford. I told my daughter that I wanted to bring her by for a visit. But I didn't, because I always seemed to be too busy. Naturally, I didn't want to miss Mama's 111th birthday or her 112th, but the sad part is that I kept driving by.

Mama died November 4, 1998, at the age of 112.

*Lalie*

# STACEY AND LAURA

*W*hen "The Chuckwagon" rolls into a Kentucky festival–Salt Lick Homecoming on Labor Day weekend in Bath County, Simon Kenton reunion in September in Mason County, Pumpkin Festival in October in Bourbon County–the first thing you'll probably notice is the cook's freshly pressed white shirt.

Then there's his tall, spotlessly white chef's hat, shoes shined, and a smile on his face for everybody. Stacey Turner's shirt and the rest of his outfit are the loving work of his wife, Laura. She's the other half of the two-person Chuckwagon management team.

Behind all that pork/beef barbecue, pork chops, and buns, and the gallons and gallons of lemonade and cola sold every year, there's a story of a man's rock-bottom despair and a woman who saw promise in an alcoholic. Back in 1978, Stacey Turner was up to a half-gallon of straight vodka every day.

"I was living from check to check, drinking visions and dreams," said Stacey in the kitchen of his and Laura's modest home in Nicholas County.

"He was hiding it everywhere. He would wake me up in the middle of the night and ask me where he'd hidden it," said Laura.

Finally she managed to have him accepted at a clinic. Stacey knew he needed professional help, and he cooperated. But it was a long way back from the bottom of the pit. He sacked groceries while Laura worked as a hairdresser. He was laid off at Christmas time through no fault of his own.

"Promise me you won't drink," Laura recalled telling Stacey. "If you do, you'll be in your grave."

A friend at Alcoholics Anonymous fixed Stacey up with a job taking in warranty parts and answering the telephone. Little by little, one day at a time, with Laura's patient help and immeasurable love, Stacey Turner climbed back to sanity and self-respect. When it came Laura's turn to lead an Al-Anon group session, she spoke of the importance of patience, causing several of the wives of alcoholics to cry, including Laura. She told them everything could be worked out with faith.

Stacey's mind began to clear. Each day he became stronger. After three months of quitting drinking, "I began to get some of my mind back. I got reality back." He'd been a shipyard pipe fitter and welder, he'd been in the Marine Corps, he'd established two beauty solons, and he'd had a couple of failed marriages. Stress, pressure, and self-pity had started him to drinking heavily when he was about thirty years old.

"It's a disease," said Laura. "He had started turning yellow. He used to go to the refrigerator and hold up a drink, and he'd say, 'I shouldn't be doing this,' and then he'd go on and do it. He was drinking his savings account."

A doctor told Stacey it was a miracle he was alive, and the doctor said he'd help only if Stacey would stop drinking. He did–cold turkey, eighteen years ago.

"I got all my marbles sort of together," said Stacey, who, after two years of operating an ice cream truck, one day decided to design and build his own chuck wagon. He and Laura bought a boat trailer for $150. They paid $15 for an old oil drum. Stacey welded. He hammered. He modified. He improvised. He worked with hardly any sleep for three months. When he finished, Stacey and Laura had enough money left "to buy two packages of hot dogs."

Laura believes in always trying to live within means. They bought a little repossessed house they could afford. They did the siding first, then the windows. They didn't buy an expensive lawnmower. "I knew we could never live in Lexington. We had to come somewhere where we could afford to live. This house is paid for. We don't ever jump into anything. Everything has to be thought out."

"She looks for deals all the time," said Stacey. "She got a good buy on that used pickup truck out there."

"Expanding the Chuckwagon?" asked Stacey. "Don't want too many working for us. We'll keep it small. If more demand is on me, I won't enjoy it. If I can make a living at my age [fifty-six in 1996], don't have to get involved with government too deep, I'll do something all day and not take a drink–and just love it."

Laura stands back from the kitchen table, and she smiles: "With labor of love, every day is payday. Rewards? The American Dream is still here if you're willing to go out there to get it."

Laura and Stacey believe that maybe this story will help somebody else.

*David*

155

# BONNIE

$\mathcal{L}$et me tell you about Bonnie Consolo.

She has no arms.

Bonnie cannot "hug," but she can embrace you with her infectious laugh and quicksilver wit. She wears a watch on her right ankle. "I'm right-footed," she says with an impish grin.

"God has given me everything I need," she says as we sit on the patio of her Louisville home on a crisp fall afternoon. She curls her big toe into the handle of the coffee mug on the table and warms both her feet as she uses them deftly to lift the hot liquid to her lips. The big city of Louisville is a long way from the little farm up a Menifee County holler. She was born there fifty-seven years ago. "My mother never treated me differently from the other four children in the family. I washed dishes, I made bread, I swept floors, I hoed the garden."

"How did you do that?"

"I held the handle between my chin and my shoulder. I worked in the house doing all the things everyone else did. When I was a baby, my mother would smack my feet if I misbehaved."

Bonnie feels at home with just about anybody. Mike Wallace with "60 Minutes" came to interview her a few years ago. After he'd asked the last question, he told the crew to call a cab for him. Bonnie said, "Don't you want me to drive you to the airport?" Without hesitation, he agreed, and off they went, Bonnie's right foot on the steering wheel.

Let Mike Wallace write stories. Bonnie Consolo has written her own history, a book called, simply, *Bonnie*. "Growing up back in the hollers gave me the right kind of beginning," she says. "We didn't have much. When you have very little you appreciate everything more."

She got her life together a long time ago and took it on the road for a national speaker's bureau. Now audiences from as far west as California and as far east as Puerto Rico appreciate Bonnie's inspirational and motivational speeches. "Parents can take a perfectly normal child and handicap them. Parents with a handicapped child should never feel sorry for that kid. That's when children start to feel sorry for themselves. A lot of parents will leave their child at home rather than go through the stares."

All the positive, inspirational advice she freely gives others doesn't mean Bonnie has not had her share of heartaches. Three failed marriages are probably enough for anyone's sense of well-being. But with grace and charm and an ironclad determination, Bonnie Consolo raised her two sons (now grown), then doggedly pursued a bachelor's degree in psychology from Morehead State University. She just graduated two years ago in May. Bonnie is the only one in her family who has a college degree.

"I went into it thinking I wanted to help other people," she says, "but I realize now that the one it has helped the most is myself. It helped Bonnie to see Bonnie. Nobody can stop me from doing anything but me. Nobody can hurt me. Now all I have to figure out is how to pay off my $18,000 student loan debt," she says with a chuckle.

Bonnie's chipping away at it. She works in customer relations for a national firm...she's taking complaints from unhappy customers who never see her but are bound to feel better just by hearing her soothing voice. On a recent weekend, Bonnie drove from Louisville to Mt. Sterling in Montgomery County to sign her book and greet old friends from the area. All day, people came to sit and chat and soak in the warmth of her wide, I-love-life smile.

Sitting in a chair with a low stool placed in front of her, with her left foot she flipped open the front pages of her book. With a pen held between the big and second toe of her right, she wrote the inscriptions with all the flair of one who has hands. A friend arrived with a new baby and Bonnie exclaimed, "Let me hold that baby!" and the mother placed the baby in Bonnie's lap. Bonnie propped the baby up against one leg and curled the other about the front of the child, who probably had never been more comfortably cradled by someone other than its mother. As the afternoon drew to a close, good-byes were exchanged and assurances were made to meet again soon. Bonnie got into her car and, smiling broadly as she drove by, lifted her right foot from the steering wheel and waved.

Note: In the summer of 1999, Bonnie was at home in Louisville. CBS' Sixty Minutes had just called and Bonnie said that she may fly to New York for another interview with Mike Wallace.

Bonnie attributes a current difficulty with her knee to flipping through the pages of her big customer service reference books while soothing customer's complaints. "My right knee was in stress and I may have tendonitis or carpal tunnel of the foot, if there is such a thing."

Bonnie's knees are, as she says, so very special and not like anyone else's. She calls her right leg "her independence," but her knee is now stiff and won't bend the way it needs to.

She'll probably have an operation to have her knee fixed. Even though Bonnie says she's having trouble with some little things that need to be done during the day, she says with a grin, "I can still wash and set my hair."

"I can still kick, but just not very high and not very hard."

*Lalie*

# FIVE WS

*S*ince nobody has called lately to ask me, "What are you reading these days?" I feel obliged to make a report.

Ordinarily I read in the evening until the cataract ("a condition in which the lens of the eye becomes progressively opaque resulting in blurred vision") in my right eye breaks down the valiant effort of the left eye to help his brother.

Early mornings are spent arm-wrestling a word processor into submission. Afternoons might find me in the stacks, the special collection rooms, and deep in the bowels of the archives of the libraries at Asbury, Lexington Theological Seminary, Transylvania, or the University of Kentucky.

I am doing what Wallace Stegner has suggested I should. I am in the process of discovering rather than constructing. It was the discovery of the beauty of the writing of Wendell Berry (*The Memory of Old Jack* and *What are People For?*) that set the stage for the discovery of Wallace Stegner (*Angle of Repose* and *The Spectator Bird*).

So, here I am, investing what's left of my cataracted right eye and my patriotic, overcompensating left eye, reading books rather than watching television. I watch it some almost unavoidably because, unlike Wendell Berry, I have not banned it from the house. Is television banning the same thing as book banning? You see, I've just discovered a new consideration, which may cause me to rethink something.

Was it Groucho Marx who said he believed television was so educational? Whoever it was said, "Whenever anybody turns on a television set, I go into the other room and read a book!"

Since I spent more than a quarter of a century taking a paycheck from commercial radio and television, it would be less than grateful to make a blanket condemnation of the technology that allowed me to watch man take his first steps on the moon.

But I should like to return to Stegner's idea of discovery first, then construction. I've been using the idea as a better way to approach the writing of a historical novel. I have patiently looked for and waited for characters, and they have been wonderful in the way they've suddenly appeared and led me to new discoveries about them and those they represent.

In life, as in writing a novel or acquiring general knowledge, if construction is foremost and discovery is second if at all, then, as my grandfather once said, there's "something wrong in your training."

If Thomas Edison had not made more than a thousand discoveries, including the microphone, phonograph, and incandescent lamp, many of us would still be constructing longer wicks for coal oil lamps and louder ways to shout. Nor would there be nearly as much magnificent music in our lives.

Dare we relate Stegner's discovery/construction idea to the educational debate?

Let's do!

After twelve years of teaching in higher education, it has at last occurred to me why I was frequently considered to be a bore, a blank piece of paper, and often the source of impractical confusion.

We live in a culture where the Bill Gateses are as vastly outnumbered as the Thomas Edisons were in the preceding century. On the nontechnological side, the Berrys and the Stegners are also in a dwindling minority. Too often, students today think (if that is the appropriate word for it) in multiple-choice stratagems and shenanigans. They dig in their mental heels when confronted with anything as obtuse as why? They are busy constructing grades and degrees.

So here we go into a new century merrily spending precious time constructing better hows rather than discovering more meaningful answers to the whys.

Is this nothing more than wordsmanship? Is this George Wallace's "pointy-headed professor" who still does not know how "to park his bicycle straight?" It is a better duty, I submit, to discover an improved balance. We can't all be Edisons, Gateses, Berrys or Stegners. But we can make a more sustained effort to discover our truest selves. If we content ourselves with being only followers along the paths of least resistance, then we become Longfellow's "dumb driven cattle."

Therefore, some questions for possible discovery:

Who are we? Why are we doing what we are doing? Where are we going and do we really want to get there? What is it all about, "Alfie?" When are we going to get off our mental rear ends and get started?

It is not by accident that I have left the how at the end of the "5-W's," where it so richly belongs. The specific how is eventually necessary, but the Who, What, When, Where, and especially the Why of our Commonwealth should be the primary considerations. Why goes to the heart of purpose; hows will be constructed after whys are revealed.

*David*

# CLEARLY LISTENING

*T*here comes the time when it no longer makes good sense to wait. Procrastination and catastrophe go hand in hand. Visibility on Plum Lick was foggy.

Now it's lifted. Cloudy conditions have been stripped away by cataract surgery.

Grandmother Nellie was totally blind most of her long life, her perpetual night probably due to a combination of procrastination, flawed diagnosis, and a void of medical technology.

As soon as the bandage came off the first day after my recent surgery, I could see reds, greens, yellows, and blues outside Central Baptist Hospital in Lexington as if they'd been turned on for the first time, just for me! I'd forgotten that we live in such a naturally textured, Technicolor world.

For a week I was told not to drive, but being co-pilot has its advantages. I was warned not to lift anything over five pounds, and that was a nice vacation too. I wore a metal patch over the recovering right eye at night to keep me from rubbing it during sleep. Having a loved one hovering and placing drops of medication, just so, became a joyful luxury. Being a good patient requires a certain amount of letting go, yet without total abdication.

On the third day of recovery, I spoke to a small group in the community room of the Middletown Public Library in Jefferson County. About six middle school students of writing were there with their teacher, repudiating the widely held perception that young people today are mainly the couch potato variety. We discussed the dangers of authoritarianism and totalitarianism, and the young insightfulness was 20/20.

On the fourth day of wondrously improving vision, I was the pronouncer for the annual spelling bee in the community room of the Paris and Bourbon County Library. The young contestants knew that the correct way to spell surgery was "s-u-r-g-E-r-y" and not "s-u-r-g-U-r-y." I'll never be confused again. It was heartening that a second grader was the runner-up in the competition. To credit KERA is probably not misplaced recognition.

On the fifth day of my new lease on sight, I spoke to about 270 people attending the annual Richmond Chamber of Commerce Awards Banquet. It happened to coincide with my wife's and my twentieth wedding anniversary. I acknowledged the mistakes as well as the triumphs in the preceding period of time and suggested that it would be the better part of profit for us all to look to the year 2018. I invited myself to be the speaker in that year. Possible mile markers might include: process over superficiality; sensitivity in gender and ethnic issues; global involvement; persistence rather than surrender; patience rather than hypertensive wheel-spinning; and goal-setting, including measured, step-by-step achievement, rather than pie-in-the-sky fantasies.

The sixth day was a Saturday and the Cynthiana DAR invited me to come and talk. Again it was the community room of the local public library. I wondered, could these spaces be best-kept secrets? Could the Kentucky Humanities Council speakers' bureau be one of the better opportunities to bring people together? Could *Kentucky Living* be one of the best bargains in reading about what invigorates and deepens the Commonwealth?

The members of the Cynthiana chapter of the Daughters of the American Revolution had requested the topic "You Can Go Home Again and Probably Should." One of my favorite notions, it's a contrarian's view of Thomas Wolfe. For him, "home" and trying to return to it was a raggedy piece of baggage. But with a new right eye working with a fairly good left one, and with a desire to reach inward for truth, outward for sharing, I found hope for the next twenty years.

On the seventh day after cataract surgery, I knew it was time to stop talking and start listening. I drove my family and myself to a little country church. It was a fine feeling being the pilot again.

We sat on the front row. The minister and I made

good eye contact. We prayed in each other's company. Later we compared medical notes. I told him I'd gone in for eye surgery and that on the seventh day I was feeling much improved. He told me he was going in for knee surgery, the better for him not only to kneel but also to walk without falling.

The minister's and my problems are rather small. We have family and friends with far graver situations. To them we say: We know, and we try each day to understand a little bit better how life is for each one of us heading on down the road.

*David*

# BITES & BYTES

$\mathcal{A}$ fundamental question is whether we desire to keep our feet firmly planted in the nineteenth or earlier centuries, or if we long to discover the new worlds of the twenty-first or later centuries. Part of the shepherd in me longs to be closely associated with Ewedawg, the Great Pyrenees puppy recently acquired at Plum Lick Farms. Ewedawg is bite, not byte, and she won't ever need a spreadsheet to tell her when a coyote or coydog needs to be sent down the road.

There's another side of the shepherd that yearns to be a part of the restless onward course of technology. There's no standing still on this one. Just as Columbus went out to discover a New World, just as Neil Armstrong took one giant step for mankind, so shepherds are ill advised to be entirely disinterested in computerization. The newest wave of advanced computer technology is multi-tasking. The old saying about not being able to do two things simultaneously is as outdated as the horse and buggy. (We're still able to respect the Amish–we just have to decide how up-to-date we need and want to be.) Even though the jury is still out on multi-tasking, there's every reason to believe that the folks at Apple, IBM, Microsoft, and other closed and locked rooms from Silicon Valley to the hidden recesses of Japan will continue to improve how it's done.

It doesn't mean we all have to multi-task all the time. There are some things better left as they are. Kissing comes to mind. So does smiling and saying "thank you." Ewedawg need not worry about protecting the shepherd as well as the sheep. That's asking too much. She's got one job to do, and as long as she does it well there's no sense in piling on another expectation.

Likewise, bigamy is against the law and there's a fairly sound basis for that. How one man could please two women or one woman please two men within a marital framework remains a mystery to most of us shepherds.

Although the Mormons took a run at polygamy in this country and may have found it to their advantage as well as their pleasure, the rest of the nation decided the better way was monogyny. Multi-spousing is out.

Then there's the problem of going forward and backward at the same time. Who needs it? One step forward and one step backward equals going nowhere. Might as well stand still in the first place. Hedging bets and straddling the issues are indications of lack of resolve and usually result in new worlds going undiscovered. Two steps forward and one step backward sure beats one step forward and two steps backward, and that may be the healthy compromise on multi-tasking. The art of compromise is probably some of the most important work at hand. To that end there's one shepherd I know who's going to keep one eye on Ewedawg and the other on what may be presently out of sight on the other side of the hill.

It seems important to hold on to what we have and try to improve the quality rather than the quantity of it. Computers and multi-tasking can help. Ideally, we can apply it in many ways–in schools, homes, churches, governmental bodies, service organizations and private institutions. Basically, we can do more of what we do best. We'll teach more skills, become more understanding in human relationships, pray more intelligently, govern more wisely, serve our communities more generously, and mind our own stores more efficiently.

This is not intended either as a panacea or as a belief that perfection is possible on this earth. Yet if every computer were unplugged, we'd probably revert to anarchy.

A world without computers might be simpler but not necessarily more efficient or even more benevolent. The word processor frees up individual creativity (remembering, however, "garbage in, garbage out"). It has the capability of increasing productivity and excellence. Graphic art is available to all those poor souls not born with the ability to draw a straight line. Spreadsheets become the roadmaps for everybody from shepherds to chief executive officers.

Ewedawg is perfection in guard dog breeding for the flock, but the shepherd needs more than one kind of help. The Great Pyrenees is an ancient breed still serving well, but the shepherds of the twenty-first century have greater, more complex, and subtler responsibilities and challenges.

*David*

# NEW BEGINNINGS

$\mathcal{I}$t happens. Just when I've sung the praises of computers. Boom! There's hardly any feeling as bad as a computer file crashing without a backup on disk. It generally happens when you least expect it. You were feeling on top of the world, flush in the glory of having created in the preceding essay an heirloom of words for immortality. Saluting Bill Gates. Doubting Wendell Berry.

As you sit there staring at a blank screen, you become as numb as a gigged frog. You feel more green and slimy and stupid than you ever thought possible. Your eyes are as round and as silent as empty saucers. You don't know how in the world you're going to re-create something that took nearly a year to accumulate. The unthinkable has just come to pass. It's close to being an ultimate free fall through the universe. There is no parachute.

You loved every word you'd written. You had poured forth your finest poetry. You had been satisfied with the rhythms of the sentences, the flow of the thoughts. Sheer poetry! The creative genie was dancing in the bottle and the dance of the seven veils was unfolding like Thomas Carew's "wise poets that wrapt Truth in tales."

All gone.

"The best of you," as Robert Service said in "The Shooting of Dan McGrew," "was to crawl away and die."

It had disappeared in a flash without a whimper, without even a "So long, it's been good to know you." You limp round about the house. You become insufferably and unforgivably sullen. Nobody's problem is as big as your problem. You are so far past hurting, there's no feeling whatsoever. There's a tendency to resign to pity, to slide back into the primordial ooze. Why would a genie be so wantonly capricious, so grossly unfair? Who is there to help?

"Fool," said my Muse to me. "Look in thy heart and write." The line from Sir Philip Sidney's sonnet reconnects me to a better self-reliance, the Emersonian kind. Yet literature alone is insufficient. My better half intercedes. She puts her arm across my shoulder, and I am encircled in an embrace that points past passion to another door of better understanding.

Imagine: Bob Dole lost, Bill Clinton's books were returned unsold, Newt Gingrich had a cellular phone problem, a prize bull calf lay down and died; a border collie lost a seven-puppy litter; the front porch is sagging; the new roof is half done; somebody didn't smile last Sunday.

As the popular song goes, it's time to pick yourself up and start all over again.

The manuscript that was lost in a cyberpit is coming back better than it was when it disappeared. It least it seems so. There's new expression in it. There's stronger vitality. Some of the "poetry" is still as lost as it so richly deserved to be. Dole, Clinton, and Gingrich had to figure what went wrong when they were gigged. They did it. Who knows, their setbacks probably improved their mortal conditions. There'll be more prize bulls and heifers and border collies. If the front porch falls all the way down, it might even look better. A leaky roof tends to remind folks that perfection is forever just over the next hill.

There are many gentle reminders that we don't have to be defeated by past mistakes. There are many chances to start over again. There's plenty of opportunity to invent new ways of doing things. Perhaps the central problem is satisfaction with the existing state of affairs. Responsibility for improvement of almost every kind begins with the individual. Without freedom, this is thwarted. It is possible too for free men and women to be creatures of their own imprisonment. We do this when we place limitations upon ourselves.

There are many roads to new destinations. There are dead ends to nowhere.

So, thank you, computer, for eating that manuscript. If it had not happened there would have been no new beginning. There would have been no new inspiration to reach out to the Carews, the Sydneys, the Emersons, even the Doles, the Clintons, and the Gingriches. There would have been continued misgivings about lost calves and puppy dogs, sagging front porches and unfinished roofs. In state government, in public and private schools, in organizations of every kind, and in our private lives, we don't have to be a pond full of frogs caught in blinding gigabytes.

*David*

# MA AND PA ON THE INTERNET

"$\mathscr{A}$ network of networks with millions of users connecting networks together–the Internet gets us where we want to go."

That's how our instructor began a recent day-long seminar I attended with my husband, who said we were there to learn all about "global E-mail," "on-line conversations," "informational retrieval" and "marketing bulletin boards." Definitely, I'm just as interested in all that New World stuff as he is, and although my female brain can run circuits through his megabytes, I try not to remind him of it.

"Honey, how about if we use some of this high tech to trace our family tree?"

"Sure," he replied, about as interested as he ever is when I suggest a little something from my corner of the cosmos. Earlier, I'd picked up the telephone and called Jim Nelson, Kentucky Department of Libraries and Archives commissioner in Frankfort. I'd asked him if I could come over and talk to him about how the Farm Bureau's *All Around Kentucky* readers could use his facility for doing a better job of tracing their family histories.

He said fine, and we set the date. My husband went along and first thing you know, the three of us were snug up to a computer monitor in Jim's office, up to our shoulder blades in things like: http://www.kdla.state.ky.us/

For those of us on the edge of the "new world," that's the computer address of how we'll all be able to go to the Kentucky Archives at 300 Coffee Tree Road without even leaving home. Certainly we can always drive over, up, or down to Frankfort if we want to–and I think we should want to–but by using the Internet and understanding its language, we can save ourselves a lot of time for darning our husbands' socks–joke, just a joke!

O.K., here we go classmates!

"Http" stands for: hyperlink technology transfer protocol.

Please don't be put off by that—"http" will become as fixed in your brain as I-64, I-75, or KERA, or HWT ("Honey, where's the...") or HWY ("Honey would you...").

The "www" part of the internet sign-on stands for "worldwide web." The "kdla" part stands for "Kentucky Department of Libraries and Archives." The "state" represents our commonwealth. The "ky" is Kentucky and "us" is the United States (all of us in the best sense of the word).

In January of 1996 we were able to access (from our homes or our community libraries or anywhere else we could find a port) such things as Civil War military records. Earlier, we could locate muster rolls, tax rolls, court and census records, criminal and civil suits, county clerks' office records, deeds, mortgages, tax assessments, will settlement books, marriages, and federal records.

Did you know Kentucky is the "Mother State" for immigration westward? Family tree trackers from the North, South, and West "have to come back here" to Kentucky, says Jim Nelson. He and his staff have been working for the last three or four months to make a home page available on the worldwide web, accessible to anyone in the world who has an internet gateway.

Stay tuned! There are new communities a-building, even a "town meeting place" for genealogists, where they can quickly obtain information about raw materials, use indexes, identify repositories, scan guide materials for libraries. There is a lot of help along the way. Joining such traditional books as Helmbold's *Tracing Your Ancestry*, there's Banner Blue's software, *Family Tree Maker*, and, according to the publication *Computer Times*, there are at least twenty-five computer user groups in the Commonwealth of Kentucky. There were really good "ancestry" ideas in a column appearing in the December 1995 issue of *Computer Times*: "It is so important to realize that life is not a rehearsal! We each have a limited number of days on this earth. It's time to begin to get the MOST from yourself TODAY!"

Exciting! You bet! We can darn a sock, trace a great-great-great grandmother, bandage a knee, and track down a great-great-great grandfather.

I know. Computers are expensive. But so are automobiles and pickup trucks. Darning needles are relatively inexpensive until you start calculating how much the darner's time is worth. Here's another idea. Let's say, none of the "https" in the computer world is for you. Let's say, computers are about as unthinkable as dancing with grizzly bears. Please, whatever you do, jot down just a little something. Put some dates that you know to be true in the family Bible. How much do you know about burial places? You can point the way to long forgotten markers. Record some information about Aunt Suzie. How tall was she? Did she smile: Did she snore? And what about Uncle Bob? Was he lean? Was he quiet? Or did he throw a fit sometimes? Don't wait for a young relative with a tape recorder to seek you out. Send out the word to them: "I want to help build a record about Kentuckians for Kentuckians!"

We'll all be the richer for it!

*Lalie*

# KINFOLKS

*O*ba Davis (pronounced "Obee," "Davis" pronounced regular) has five daughters–Nancy, Tommye, Martha Ann, Rose, and Jeanne. They never waited for a man to tell them that they needed to do something for themselves. Oba always said she wanted her daughters "to have their own business," that it was "better than working for somebody else."

Mama Oba remembers how hard her husband worked to haul hay from Liberty in Casey County to Hazard in Perry County, or Manchester in Clay County. He'd sell it to farmers who had cows to feed and return with coal for folks at home to keep their hearth warm in winter.

"Daddy's been dead twenty-one years. He'd be so proud of us," says Nancy.

Now, with the five daughters, eleven grandchildren and fourteen great-grandchildren, Oba is the inspiration for a place of business on U.S. 127 about one mile south of Liberty. It's called "Kinfolk Treasures."

> *Kinfolks are life's treasures*
> *Be they far or near*
> *Memories of times together*
> *Hearts we hold so dear.*
>
> *Copyright © Kinfolk Treasures*

Drop by sometime and meet eighty-one-year-old Oba, her daughters, and other members of the family. You don't have to buy anything in order to feel welcome. Arm-twisting is not their style. Kinfolk Treasures opened May first just in time for Mother's Day four years ago, and now the word has spread up and down the U.S. 127 "corridor" from Cincinnati to Alabama.

"How many times we've been told by travelers," says Nancy, "that they go south by I-65 or I-75 and return by U.S. 127." The scenic route begins at

Lake Cumberland and goes through Liberty, Danville, Harrodsburg, Lawrenceburg, Frankfort, Owenton, and Big Bone Lick.

"We knew what we had to do," says Tommye. "We pooled our money, paid our rent, and kept selling faster than we could make."

"We all had things we'd made at home, and we brought them down here to sell," says Nancy. "We all had a job and we worked at home at night."

"Scared to death at first?"

"Still scary. It's scarier now because we don't have a job. We can't get sick. Our husbands say we fuss if we don't have any business, whine if we do."

"Any major disagreements?"

"We've always been real close. Each one does her own thing, and we usually agree on just about everything. If we don't, we just work it out. Whoever's the busiest stays with it, the other goes out front."

"Mama makes Raggedy Ann and Andy and sock monkeys. Mama makes bonnets and aprons. Mama makes useful stuff." The daughters defer to their mother, and their love and respect show and sound as clear as a bell. They also keep alive the memory of their father. The cedar wardrobe he made is right there in the shop. "A part of him is here," says Tommye. "He'd be so proud of us."

One of Kinfolks' "for sale" treasures is a three-way bonnet–folds out to make a small apron, gathers in to hold clothesline pins, folds in to shade any lady's pretty face. "When I was a child, women wore bonnets to match their aprons," says Oba. Clothespins also make wonderful angels. You can be a collector of angels, all kinds, from Amish girls to cheerleaders. And then there's the baby sack filled with "Itty Bitty Christians": five tiny fabric "children" tucked inside for little ones to take to church to play with while their parents are busy praying.

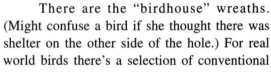

There are the "birdhouse" wreaths. (Might confuse a bird if she thought there was shelter on the other side of the hole.) For real world birds there's a selection of conventional birdhouses. There are "spool dolls," stick horses, dowel rod creations, handmade baskets, and jar candles. Mama does "little rips and alterations" on the side. It's enough to keep three sewing machines humming.

Next time you're down at Gatlinburg, Tennessee, at the "God's Country" gift shop, you might be interested in knowing that some of the crafts were created at Kinfolk Treasures in Casey County, Kentucky. And should you be planning to motor north or south on U.S. 127, you might want to mark your calendar for the Liberty Apple Festival in the last full week of September. That's when they celebrate the "World's Largest Apple Pie." It's free to the public. ("Mama makes the best fried apple pies" in case the "World's Largest" gives out.)

"I love to work," says Oba Davis, "and I love my family...I don't see how people sit idle."

The number-one best seller at Kinfolk Treasures?

Angels.

"I think it's helped Mama stay younger," says Nancy.

"I've worked all my life," says Oba, "And I've not got a lazy child."

"How does the future look?"

"Hope it's good," says Oba, looking up from her repair work on a little boy's overalls.

*Lalie*

# MICKEY

*W*hen Medra Hays lost her husband nine years ago, she was broken-hearted. "I sat and cried for four months after Rodney died," she said as she dipped her bookbinder's brush into a large jar of glue. Her wrist moved smoothly as she applied the adhesive to the open spine of a volume tattered with age and use.

"This is what I need to do. Have to do it for my emotions. It brought me through it," said Medra "Mickey" Hays, owner of Hays Bookbinding, possibly (in 1996) the last business of its kind in the Commonwealth of Kentucky. Mickey practices a vanishing art in a time of mainly disposable consumer products: use it, toss it; damage it, never mind repairing it; grow tired of it, buy something new.

Orphaned as a child in the mountains of Eastern Kentucky, adopted by a kind lady at Midway College, Mickey, now sixty-five years old, continues to work at home in Fayette County. She says she's slowing down after thirty-one years of repairing damaged volumes for the state archives in Frankfort, the City of Lexington, the Kentucky Water Company, and the Veteran's Hospital. She binds doctoral dissertations for the University of Kentucky.

Perhaps the most personal and enriching work Mickey does is restoring the frayed and broken backs and covers of Bibles owned by individuals and families, those for whom something "new" completely misses the point.

"I put my whole self into it," said Mickey in her tiny shop, where the summer air blows through the open door, and memories of her late husband, long-time Transylvania University biology professor Rodney Hays, are seldom far away.

"We made a lab out of the dining room. We ate on one end of the table and did research on the other end. We had 3,000 salamanders in jars...he had scientific journals stacked from the floor to the ceiling."

When Mickey wondered out loud how all these journals could be bound, her husband brought home "how-to" books. Professor Hays (his academic career stretched over three decades at Transylvania) encouraged Mickey to become what she is today–one of the last of Kentucky's bookbinders. She recalls attending special classes, but there was hardly any substitute for doing what she'd always known best: rolling up her sleeves and going to work. This was the beginning of the little company, Hays Bookbinding, where today there's one full-time employee and she's her own boss.

She drills the holes, feathers the pages with a hammer and handmade presses, cuts the mulls (cloth hinges) and the book boards, measures for the lettering on the covers, sets type, stamps the characters, adds new front and end pages, and keeps the glue jar jumping.

"If you find a mistake, bring it back and I'll fix it for nothing," Mickey tells her customers. She says her re-bound books are "put together to stay."

Since Mickey Hays likes to work with her hands, it's natural that she undertakes a few odd jobs over at the house, when she isn't binding books– well, just a little thing or two, here and there.

"...tore out the floor, commode, and tank in my bathroom and replaced it;

"...removed all the cabinets from my kitchen and with the help of my cousin put in 'new ones' brought from another kitchen;

"...built a back porch onto my house twenty years ago, just replaced a post this week; the other one rotted out;

"...my seven-year-old granddaughter and I made earrings using buttons, a hobby she likes;

"...added a 20' x 20' patio;

"...built plastic-covered frames to insert during winter or rain, so the porch can be dry and not so cold;

"...for my son's birthday [Mickey and Rodney have three children], I built a 6'-wide TV center with places for a VCR, tapes, and a book shelf...

"...sometimes I can repair my push lawn mower and do little repairs on my riding mower [she mows about two and a-half acres of grass all summer];

"...my daughter picks up broken-down furniture from the side of the road for garbage pickup, brings it to me to overhaul, and then she gives it to people she knows who need it. I just completed a chest of drawers for her and am about to make two drawers that are missing from a chest;

"...do cake decorating, especially wedding cakes...occasionally I do the complete reception;

"...I work with Midway alumni to help girls in need."

Oh, one other thing. Mickey used to make her husband's and children's clothes. Now, with a little time on her hands, she's taken all her late husband's suits and cut them into squares:

"I'm making wool quilts with flannel linings. I have to add to the wool to bring out colors I need. I've given three to our children, four to former students, two to our best neighbors, one to a former judge who is our special friend, and seven more for special reasons. My first cousin just received one. I've made seventeen quilts in all so far."

For Medra "Mickey" Hays, the bookbinder, the Jill of all trades, working in her shop and house could be a recipe for loneliness and a broken heart. She calls it her "peaceful solitude."

In May of 1999, despite two strokes in recent years, Mickey Hays was still in her shop, answering the phone and binding books.

*Lalie*

# GLADYS

*A* few years ago, I took a little trip to taste the home cooking down at the McKinney Depot Restaurant in Lincoln County, and I'm here to tell you, Gladys Reed knew how to get the job done. With her, running a restaurant is a lot more than a job–it's a love. When I talked with her to update her story for *Home Sweet Kentucky*, she told me she'd moved over to Stanford to open a new restaurant, Kentucky Depot. Gladys said another couple was running the McKinney Depot Restaurant, so maybe that's another story for another time.

Here's how it was when I visited Gladys Reed before she left McKinney and moved to Stanford.

After a twenty-year career as a hair stylist, she had switched tracks to plunge headlong into the restaurant business. People drove considerable distances just for a slice of her brown sugar pie. Sometimes, especially on Mother's Day, there'd be a hungry line of cars parked on Busy Bee Street to Main to the Post Office in McKinney, present population about 300, give or take a few.

One of the early settlements in Kentucky, McKinney Fort was founded in 1789. The Norfolk & Southern freights run through where, long before Daniel Boone, prehistoric Native Americans once hunted for something good to eat. No telling how they might have carried on about Gladys Reed's marinated fried chicken or her "melt-in-your-mouth" tenderloin or her Friday night batter-free, flame-grilled catfish, or her deep-fried okra, or her creamed peas, or her corn fritters, or her yeast rolls. Oh, those yeast rolls! (Gladys let me make off with her recipe and she said I could share it with you. It's at the end of the story.)

"I never cut a corner...if [a recipe] calls for six cups of sour cream, I use six cups," she says, emphatically.

The main thing about Gladys is her commitment to what she does, actually what she's dreamed of doing since she was a little girl. "I was always in the kitchen. I love good food...nothing fancy...anything I can make from scratch, I do," says Gladys while taking a short breather from the kitchen. When I dropped by, she was right in there with the employees, eight to ten in the kitchen plus seven waitresses and four hostesses.

"I oversee all the cooking. I know what things are supposed to taste like. I'm here all the time, seven days a week, and the food is consistently good."

With her husband, Danny, and their two teenage sons, Joe Dan and John David (and, yes, they do help with the dishes), Gladys and her team have worked hard. She told me they satisfied the appetites of an average 1,000 to 1,100 customers a week (250 to 300 on Sundays).

The last I heard, there were two choices–McKinney Station, under new management, or Glady's new place at the junction of US. 27 and US 150 in Stanford. Take your pick. Since the directions to McKinney Station are kind of fun, I'd like to let them stand as written after my first trip down that way.

Letting your taste buds be your guide and using Danville as a starting point, the best way to find McKinney is to head south to Stanford, where you'll pick up KY 78. Go 4.9 miles to KY 198. Turn left there and go 2.8 miles to McKinney. If you overshoot KY 198 and wind up in Chicken Bristle, don't worry. Just turn left at Chicken Bristle and go south on KY 3250 to McKinney. Six of one, half a dozen of the other. As you come into McKinney, you'll pass Boneyard Hollow Road, another one of those smiley-faced Kentucky reference points. Just past Boneyard Hollow road, turn right onto Main Street and go one block to Busy Bee Street, turn left, and the place you've come for is on the right. Next to it, when I dropped in, there was a bright red caboose, which Gladys used for a gift shop. She had another gift shop inside, presided over by her first cousin Connie Henderson.

When I was there, I could sit in a swing or in a rocking chair on the long porch and prop my feet on the railing to watch and feel the vibrations of the Norfolk & Southern freights lumbering past. The engineers sounded a friendly toot on the whistle to say hello to me, which was nice. Gladys recalled how her husband, Danny, had to retire as a conductor after he was hurt in a truck accident.

Before this sounds too much like a commercial for a restaurant, let me tell you why I decided to do this story. Gladys Reed, I think, is a good woman, a good wife, a good mother, and a good individual who stands on her own two feet and makes a difference. It doesn't matter whether she's in McKinney or Stanford.

"Nowadays," says Gladys, "parents feel like they can't control things...I tell my kids, 'Don't feed your brains with this stuff–the bad movies, the bad language. Your brain is like a computer; it's going to come back out.' I sit on the bed and talk to them...when my eighteen-year-old came in (recently) he woke me up and kissed me and told me goodnight. Danny doesn't go to bed until they come in.

"Danny and I have had a perfect marriage, twenty-three years. We've always had a lot of respect for one another."

Are they making a lot of money?

"We're the wealthiest people in the world when it comes to life."

### Gladys Reed's Recipe for Yeast Rolls

2 pkgs. dry yeast
2 cups lukewarm water
1/2 cup sugar
2 teaspoons salt
6-1/2 to 7 cups bread flour
1 egg
1/4 cup vegetable oil

Dissolve yeast in water. Add sugar, salt, & half of the flour. Mix until moist. Mix egg & oil together then stir into flour & yeast mixture. Add remaining flour & mix well. Place in oiled bowl to rise. Punch down, roll out 1/2" thick, cut with biscuit cutter, dip in melted butter or margarine, fold over, seal with a finger poke, let rise once more on baking pan. Bake at 400 degrees for 12 minutes.

*Lalie*

# JESSE

*J*esse Stuart is alive in the Jesse Stuart Foundation.

The foundation, which Jesse authorized in 1979, five years before his death, is a public, nonprofit organization "devoted to preserving both Jesse Stuart's literary legacy and W-Hollow, the little valley made famous in his works."

That's important because Jesse Stuart is a starting point for Kentucky readers and writers in the next century. His commitment alone to a lifetime of teaching makes him a necessity.

It's a misjudgment to dismiss Jesse as a prolific primitive who shares no place with a Wendell Berry, a Barbara Kingsolver, a Bobbie Ann Mason, or a Robert Penn Warren. It would be a mistake to substitute Stuart for the prodigious work of these exceptional talents of the present time. But, Jesse is bedrock. Berry, Mason, Kingsolver, and Warren are, shall we say, the occupants of the book-lined shelves of the front room.

Here's a way, perhaps, of understanding Jesse Stuart better. It comes in a fine, indispensable little volume published in 1988 by the Jesse Stuart Foundation. The book–*Jesse Stuart: The Man and His Books*–includes a useful chronology of the Kentuckian most often remembered as the author of the best-selling *Taps for Private Tussie* (1943) and *The Thread That Runs So True* (1949), which is still in print; my personal copy is the twenty-seventh edition.

Jesse Stuart's "first commercially published book," *Man with a Bull-Tongue Plow*, appeared in 1934. The author was only twenty-eight-years old. Of this landmark book the late Jim Wayne Miller has written: "Like Whitman, Jesse Stuart had eyes to see, ears to hear, and the literary ability to portray and interpret his own land and people."

Miller, in an essay appearing in *Jesse Stuart: The Man: and His Books,* wrote: "Stuart was not the sort of trendy, fashionable writer, anxiety-ridden and alienated, who fancied himself too deep and sensitive to be understood. Stuart's work is accessible. He did not stand back from the common life; he plunged into it."

I confess that, when I read Jesse's first novel, *Trees of Heaven* (1940), I was dreadfully put off by what I thought was its awkward, first-person excessiveness. Now I know it's a mistake to judge any man by one book. Likewise, what I saw in *Taps for Private Tussie*–stereotypes feeding an insatiable appetite of Ivy League and Madison Avenue readerships–was missing the main value of Jesse Stuart's legacy.

An essay by Jerry A. Herndon, "Jesse Stuart's World," (*Journal of Kentucky Studies*, 1984) is reprinted in *Jesse Stuart: The Man and His Books*: "His people live in interdependent rural communities, yet they are also independent, self-reliant individuals."

And there is the nub of it. That is the message to take home and nail to the wall. Jesse Stuart predates the high-tech classroom. There's hardly any avoiding electronic teaching devices these days, but any teacher, superintendent, school board member, parent, or student who has not read *The Thread That Runs So True* (Charles Scribner's Sons, New York) should find a copy and turn to page 197. To paraphrase: Whatever you decide to do in life, do it the best you're able. When you teach, remember those who are least able to learn. Teach them that they can be an important credit to their community.

Probably Jesse Stuart should be remembered most of all because he was a teacher. When I visited his gravesite in the Plum Grove Cemetery in Greenup County, I read the words and saved them:

'No one can ever tell me that education, rightly directed without propaganda, cannot change the individual, community, county, state, and the world for the better. It can...and I am firm in my belief that a teacher lives on and on through his students....Good teaching is Forever and the teacher is immortal."

One of the main threads that runs so true through the fabric of Kentucky and the rest of the world is books. Videos and electronic texts are branches on the tree of learning, hardly replacements for volumes of life that nurture ideas. *Jesse Stuart: The Man and His Books* is a guide through a landscape growing more confused every day with the "information explosion."

Jim Wayne Miller said of Jesse Stuart: "He was instinctively positive, an affirmer....Because he was both a dreamer and a doer, he turned his dreams into deeds and words. He did not tear down. He was a builder–of barns, fences, and land. And he was a builder with words."

James M. Gifford, Executive Director of the Jesse Stuart Foundation, is a caring man who can be reached at the following address: P.O. Box 391, Ashland, Kentucky 41114.

*David*

# GLENNIS & WHITEY

$\mathcal{W}$-Hollow in northeast Greenup County lies at the end of a road that winds like a peaceful ribbon among the hills now covered with bare trees and carpets of fallen leaves. This is Jesse Stuart country, known internationally through the teaching and writing of its famous native son. Jesse died in 1984, but Jesse's baby sister is well on her way to becoming famous in her own right.

"I'm a cooking fanatic," laughs Glennis Stuart Liles as she leads the way into her warm home filled with the aroma of good things to come. "We've fixed a few things for lunch out of my cookbooks."

Sitting with Glennis and her husband, Whitey, in their cozy living room, we listen as she spins the tale of how her cookbooks came to be. In the telling of the story, it's apparent that these aren't just any cookbooks. They're cookbooks with an unselfish purpose.

"I wrote to family members and asked them for their best tried-and-true recipes. We paid for all the typing and gathered the photographs for the book," says Glennis. But then, she explains, she did something that was completely unconventional. She donated the whole kit and caboodle–a collection of more than a thousand categorized, tested recipes–to the Jesse Stuart Foundation. Why would anyone, after going to all that expense and effort, want to give away a project that enormous or that potentially profitable?

"I have a great love for my brother and his writing," says Glennis. "All the income from the sale of the books goes to the foundation to finance production of Jesse's books. Keeping his books in print was the inspiration for doing it. I'd never done anything like it before."

James Gifford, director of the Jesse Stuart Foundation, says they'd never seen anything like it before either. "We sold out of the first edition in two months," he says. "Historically, the *W-Hollow Cookbook* and the eight Jesse

Stuart Junior Books have been our most successful books." The *W-Hollow Cookbook* is now in its third edition.

There's also *W-Hollow Holidays and Holiday Recipes*, a month-by-month collection of fond memories and holiday ideas to prepare. "I asked the family for recipes they've used over and over for holidays, so some of these recipes are over 150 years old."

How do you know when a cooking idea is a good one? Glennis says you can tell "just by the sound of it," but that doesn't mean that any recipe passes without some good, old-fashioned taste testing. When she was compiling the first cookbook, she and her niece, Betty Stuart Baird, categorized all the recipes and tested those that sounded doubtful. "One day we cooked twenty-five dozen cookies and Betty's husband was the tester," Glennis laughs. "We've never had a complaint."

Whitey's main job is doing the dishes, but he's a cook of some repute as well. When he reads a recipe, he says the "first thing I do is draw up a sinkful of hot, soapy water. I like to clean as I go."

The couple shares kitchen space pretty much as you'd expect of couples married forty-eight years next February 5. "We get in each other's way," Glennis says with a chuckle. "If I want in that drawer, he's standing in the way. If he wants in this cabinet, I'm in the way. I have considered retreating sometimes."

Just being in their company, I could tell these two really enjoy working well and unselfishly together. Others have recognized Glennis and Whitey's penchant for giving. In 1997, an Ashland television station, after receiving a petition from more than 150 neighbors, named them "Hometown Heroes" for their contributions during the floods that devastated Greenup County.

"We cooked everything–big pots of soup and chili–we fixed breakfast, fixed evening meals. Every room in our house had someone staying in it part-time. When one bunch moved out, there'd be another bunch to move in. We even had a special room for the cats and dogs," laughs Glennis. But then she says somberly of the flood victims: "There were those who'd just stand on the Little Sandy River bank and cry."

Glennis and her siblings, Sophie, Jesse, Mary, and James, knew hardship and how to rise above it firsthand. "You can do anything you want to do. I think Jesse proved that. Maybe my whole family proved that because there wasn't anyone more poor then we were. My dad bought this place in 1918 for $350 and got it paid for in 1935. He almost lost it twice, but we grew what we ate and we all pulled together and," she says proudly. "The five children that lived to be grown all graduated from college, some with masters' degrees,  and all were successful."

Glennis graduated from Lincoln Memorial University, then taught for thirty-three years in the Greenup County school system. She's still teaching-teaching with recipes for unselfishness and love for family.

*Lalie*

# ANOTHER BRIDGE TO THE PAST

*R*emember me?

I'm a covered bridge.

Once we numbered more than four hundred here in Kentucky. Now there are only thirteen of us–the final thirteen.

The Yatesville covered bridge over Blaine Creek in Lawrence County near the Big Sandy River collapsed during a storm in 1986 to become the latest victim of both age and shameful neglect. The Yatesville Bridge–leaning and sagging–was built in 1879 and was in use until 1965. "Only a matter of time," says Gene Marvin, editor of the *Big Sandy News*.

There used to be three of us within a distance of less than three miles on the Thatcher's Mill Road in Bourbon County–one over Stoner Creek, one over Strode's Creek, and one over Pretty Run Creek. We didn't collapse. The Department of Highways tore us down and replaced us with squeaky clean concrete spans. Local residents, I'm told, were tickled to death. They said they thought we were hazardous, especially in wintertime. That puzzles me. Even out on the big super interstate highways nobody raises an eyebrow about the need for signs that warn: "Bridge May Ice Over Before Roadway."

What really possessed our friends to destroy us? Was it safety? Or was it convenience? Maybe it was a desire to be modern. We were willing to move aside in the name of progress to accommodate folks bent on driving faster to arrive at their destinations in less time. We know how all-fired important that is today–heck fire, it's not patriotic to be opposed to safety. But couldn't there have been a way to build near us rather than through us? Did we really have to be ripped out like a bad sore?

Maybe on a Sunday a child might have said, "What is that funny looking thing over there?" Maybe parents would have slowed down and said, "That's a covered bridge. Would you like to stop and look at it? Would you like to run your hands over the wood? Smell it? How about a picnic there next Sunday?"

The reality is, these children will never know the pleasure of walking through a covered bridge on the Thatcher's Mill Road. If they somehow find out about it, maybe they'll ask their parents, "Why did you let them do that?"

To be listed on the National Register of Historic Places should be cause for reassurance, but we covered bridges know better than that.

Shortly after the Civil War the Sherburne Bridge–built at a cost of $3,500–was a vital link on the old stagecoach route between Mt. Sterling and Maysville. In 1975 a new concrete bridge was built at the Bath and Fleming County lines, and the Sherburne Bridge–in use for more than a hundred years–became even more dignified in retirement. How proud and picturesque was this historic spot–until two youths set the old Sherburne Covered Bridge afire the night of April 6, 1981. Now only the naked abutments are left standing.

Another child might say, "What is that funny looking thing over there?" A traveler on Highway 11 might say, "That's where a covered bridge used to stand."

Of the remaining thirteen covered bridges in Kentucky, one is in Bourbon County. I'm called the Colville Bridge. I'm 110 years old and still in use. But please don't bring your child over here to see me. I'm embarrassed and I'm sure you will be too. You see, I've been spray-painted with obscenities and other graffiti from one end to the other and top to bottom.

Bourbon County Sheriff Charles Ransdell will tell you how bad it is out here almost any weekend night when the weather is fine. "Hundreds of arrests" have been made, mostly for public intoxication, but marijuana smoking is another favorite pastime. I just don't understand why anybody would want to turn me into a New York subway art gallery for star-spangled, multicolored four-letter words.

The Boy Scouts came out to see me. I sure was glad to see them. For a while I was a little less embarrassed. The scouts painted over my portals and I didn't look so hideous. But after my young friends had departed, the usual crowd returned to drink beer and smoke marijuana and repaint me with nasty words as bad as ever before.

We covered bridges are mainly forgotten. That's why I'm so grateful for my good friend Vernon White, who has written a splendid book, *Covered Bridges: Focus on Kentucky*, published in 1985 by Kentuckie Imprints of Berea. It includes a very useful bibliography. I'll leave you for now with some of Vernon White's words:

"It has been a pleasure to try and preserve, in writing, the work of the honest, skilled craftsman of the 1800's. A good citizen should save for posterity that which will not again be reproduced."

*David*

# JANICE

*I*'m so sorry I never met Janice Holt Giles, but I feel as if I've known her through her writing. As time goes on, I see that she must have been writing about herself in the personages of the women who were strong and endured so much to make the state what it is. Or maybe she and I want to be like them. To me, Janice is a woman's woman, a Kentuckian's Kentuckian.

Standing with my daughter at the Gileses' graveside at the Caldwell Church cemetery at the top of that gentle hill in Adair County, I paused a moment and said a prayer. It was a hope that my daughter and all her generation would discover the magic of the woman who wrote so clearly and so well about the adopted land she loved.

Up and down the ridges east of Knifley, the dogwoods were in bloom and Spout Springs Branch shimmered past the Giles cabin with a sound as delicate as the trill of the unseen bird nearby. The woman who wrote all those fine books–*The Kentuckians, The Enduring Hills, The Believers* and, I suppose, my favorite, *Hannah Fowler*–would not have been cheered by what I saw that day I stopped by.

The bedroom was bare, and only a picture of the four-poster bed was tacked to the wall. All of the rooms were empty. I kept hoping to see something to remind me of Janice seated at her writing place, but there was no desk, no typewriter. And the kitchen cried out for cooking. "The kitchen was the priceless room to me, the heart of the home," Janice wrote in *A Little Better than Plumb.*

Charlie Sparks had led us up from Columbia to look inside where once there was so much amazing creativity. He's one of the volunteers who helps in the project to try to save the place, the three cabins joined like the big pieces of a child's puzzle, and the impoundment of water where the lily pads thrive a little too well. Charlie knows time is running out, but he doesn't give up the good fight. The end of the month of May is the deadline for raising the funds necessary to complete the purchase of the property. The Giles Foundation (P.O. Box 932, Columbia, KY 42728) is coordinating this and the planting of trees and the development of programs for schools, churches, and civic groups.

Janice died June 1, 1979. But her twenty-four books live on in first editions and reprints by the University Press of Kentucky (titles east of the Mississippi River). There are those who believe the idea of "a little better than plumb" deserves to be more than just the title of one of the four books Janice says she worked on with her husband, Henry. He's buried beside her up in the Caldwell Church cemetery. The simple words on the headstone are a reminder that he was a sergeant in World War II.

I walked with my daughter through the part of the Giles house that once was the church of a black congregation. The tiny choir loft is still intact. "Logs a hundred fifty years old are still alive. They aren't dead. They are a little restless and they move slightly and they speak."

Thirty-five years later, another car approaches. A man and his wife from Eubank are leading a couple from Brodhead to visit the old Giles homestead. Charlie invites them in and tells them what he knows about the place, slowly falling apart unless there are more volunteers to pitch in and help rebuild the porches and reinforce the chinking of the great logs. "The logs have heard a lot of laughter, a lot of good talk, a lot of fine music, few harsh words and almost no weeping."

Now a large piece of the tin roof curls back and threatens to fly away even when the wind is gentle. There's so much work to be done! It's one thing to preserve the evidence of a piece of Kentucky heritage, and I support it with all my heart and some of my pocketbook, but that alone is not the main thought in my mind. Janice would not have wanted just the preservation of the cabin where she and Henry lived and loved and worked. Even her monument is small and stands at the back of the cemetery, where so many Giles family members have been laid to rest. She wanted nothing fancy.

Most of all, I believe Janice would have wanted the present generation's recognition and respect for the real characters in her books. Simply that and nothing more.

*Lalie*

# JANE AND JIM

*T*he house on Shelby Street in Frankfort sits–no, it soars; no, it breathes–within a stone's throw of the Capitol.

Frank Lloyd Wright would be proud. After all, he designed it. It's the only house in Kentucky created by the genius who conceived more than four hundred structures throughout the world, including the magnificent Guggenheim Museum of Art in New York City and the earthquake-proof Imperial Hotel in Tokyo.

The Capitol in Frankfort, completed in 1910, bordered (according to local lore) on land that once was a farm. The farmhouse was torn down to make room for a plat of residential lots, and the first structure built was the house that Wright built. He designed it as one of his prairie-style residences: openness through multiple windows; to be "better contained" by optimum use of space; unity achieved by melding "inside" with "outside" through nature; but, most importantly to Plum Lickers, a feeling of continuing life.

Enter Jane and Jim Brockman.

Jane answered the door. (Actually, Mille, the protective schnauzer, was the first to greet the visitors and the last to see them on their way to the car.) Jane's husband, Jim joined her, and the tour began.

First we sat in the living room and looked at albums of pictures of the family of Frankfort Presbyterian minister J.R. Zeigler, who paid $5,000 to have the house built in 1910. Reverend Zeigler met Frank Lloyd Wright, according to the historical marker outside, "on a voyage to Europe," but there's no documentation of the exact location of the meeting. In any event, Mr. Wright agreed to be the architect. Much later, in the company of Louisville Mayor Charles Farnsley, Wright paid a visit to the house on Shelby Street.

The Brockmans, who know a thing or two about restoration in general and Frank Lloyd Wright in particular, purchased the house in 1991 after several other families had lived in it. Jane and Jim undertook an extensive and detailed renovation of each room, each inch of wall covering. They carefully researched replacements for each piece of furniture to make 1910 live all over again.

"The kids thought we'd lost our minds," said Jane, as she rubbed Mille's well-tended schnauzer coat. The kids are grown now and have begun their own lives. "We sold our house and medical building in Owensboro," said Jim. "Everything we have is in this house, our own resources, no borrowed money."

A Frank Lloyd Wright house typically puzzles as much as it thrills, but the key to the visit on a hot summer day thirty-six years after the death of the master architect lay in the hands of Jane and Jim Brockman. Without their patience and love, the house might have gone the way of so many other priceless landmarks, facing misuse and eventual destruction, and finally replacement, perhaps with something "modern."

Jim, a pharmacist from Owensboro, had dreamed since boyhood the Frank Lloyd Wright dream. That dream came true when he and Jane discovered the house just down the slope from the Kentucky Capitol. They sold the business and made the move. They spent $25,000 just to strip the woodwork, which had darkened with age. Restored to its original luster, the mantle above the living room fireplace and the lighted rectangular case reaching to the ceiling produce a stunning and pleasing effect. The Brockmans believe it was what Frank Lloyd Wright had in mind.

The leaded glass windows that wrap the living room and dining area create a feeling of "outside being inside," an architectural style pioneered by Wright. He liked to call it "organic," meaning kinship with nature,

a word that he preferred to capitalize–Nature.

The furniture in the house at the time of our visit in 1995 was Victorian. While it might not have pleased Mr. Wright, the Brockmans believe it is in keeping with the Zeigler family's tastes.

Not every trip away from Plum Lick leads to Frank Lloyd Wright architecture, Victorian furniture, or people as gracious and unselfish as Jane and Jim Brockman. About four thousand people have tramped through the house that sits–no, soars, no, breathes–on Shelby Street in Frankfort, a private home with a public heart.

One visitor, who saw Jane eating lunch there one day, declared, "Who are you?"

Jane answered, "I live here."

The lady who lives in this home sweet Kentucky home has a recipe for happiness: "We have always been very frugal people, always saved. There's no such thing as luck, but luck is where opportunity meets preparation."

Frank Lloyd Wright is alive and well in Frankfort, Kentucky.

*David*

# FATHER LOUIS

*A*s a child growing up in Kentucky, I'd heard of the monks living at the Abbey of Gethsemani in Nelson County. From the beginning, they filled me with wonderment. How could they do such a thing? How could they walk away from a world I'd only begun to savor?

My family was unaware of Thomas Merton's towering autobiography, *The Seven Storey Mountain*, which skyrocketed to the bestseller list in 1948, the year I graduated from high school. We were still too busy recovering from the traumas of World War II, too caught up in the Fabulous Five and the University of Kentucky's first national basketball championship, too mesmerized by Joe Louis knocking out Jersey Joe Walcott.

Now, after more wars, more basketball titles, more knockdowns and knockouts, as I approach three score and nine, I find myself in better harmony with Thomas Merton and the other Trappist monks, alive and buried, at the Abbey of Gethsemani.

A new acquaintance in Bardstown, Don Parrish, offered to take me down to see for the first time the oldest Trappist monastery in the United States. Don's father was a carpenter for the building of Father Louis's hermitage (Louis was Thomas Merton's name at Gethsemani), where he lived in solitude, where he wrote and became internationally famous.

After we'd visited the austere church, Don Parrish and I went to the main information desk where a monk seemed as much at home with modern communications as he was with the expectations of silence in cloistered living.

"May we visit the cemetery of the monks?" Don asked.

"Why would you want to do that?" inquired the monk with a friendly smile.

"My friend would like to visit the grave of Father Louis," said Don.

"Go through that door and walk straight ahead," said the monk with a voice as pleasant as it was helpful.

We walked up to the knoll where the Trappists sleep in what might be called the profoundest of peace, the graves marked with simple iron crosses, each bearing a name and a date of death. Father Louis passed away about thirty years ago but his writings, under the name Thomas Merton, live on. There was an indescribable hush on the day I stood beside the grave and lightly touched the iron marker, a feeling of joy I'd not known before.

The next day, I did what I knew I must. I returned with my wife to the Abbey of Gethsemani so that she too could experience the church where services begin at 3:30 in the morning. At midday, we prayed together. Then we went to ask again for permission to visit Thomas Merton's final resting-place.

"My wife would like to see it," I said to the same monk who had greeted me the day before. He did not ask, "Why would you want to do that?"

"Of course, you may," he said. "You know the way?"

"Yes, I do," I said, and we walked to the spot where Father Louis was waiting for us.

There were no words.

In the days that followed, I bought Diane April's new book, *The Abbey of Gethsemani, Place of Peace and Paradox: 150 Years in the Life of America's Oldest Trappist Monastery.* It is a beautiful work, and we shall always treasure it.

I also have begun rereading *The Seven Storey Mountain* and at long last I've begun reading the journals of Thomas Merton. While I most likely will never become a Trappist monk at the Abbey of Gethsemani, the texture of the lives behind those walls and out in those fields will quite possibly encourage me to seek peace before war, education more than slam-dunks, haymakers, and a little bingo on the side.

Three score and nine bring many trials, and it's not easy to say which is the greatest. But whatever the age–youth, young adult, middle age, or beyond–we all have the opportunity to move forward toward the discovery of our truest, best selves.

It becomes a matter of contemplation, does it not? Our understanding of that reality is most likely all the reward Thomas Merton ever dreamed of having.

*David*

# SISTER MARY JANE

*S*he was born on a farm in Nelson County in the parish of St. Thomas, not too far from the place where the Sisters of Charity first established their order.

In 1939, she came to the Sisters of Charity of Nazareth, Kentucky, and that's where you'll find Sister Mary Jane today–teaching and painting and sculpting.

Greeting us at the front door of the stately old O'Connell Hall, Sister Mary Jane led us up the ancient staircase to the second floor and into a spacious room filled with soft, natural light filtering through tall, gracefully arched windows–an artist's dream studio.

There were so many colorful quilts and pieces of fiber art displayed in the great room that Sister Mary Jane explained, "We're having a show on Saturday and I'm going to be throwing some pots on my wheel."

Motioning us toward a long table covered with colorful fabric and surrounded by easels holding paintings she and her students had done, she recalled growing up on the farm with six brothers and six sisters, and her life as a nun.

Her mother and father worked hard to support the family back in the days of the Great Depression when moonshining made an important difference.

"It was the only cash people had. My parents were 'artists' with a great deal of pride, artists in that they knew so many things about nature. My father knew about trees. When we walked with him, he pointed out the different kinds–maple, oak, and locust. We had to do things. My mother was a seamstress. She preserved hundreds of jars of food. There was a great deal of pride. When my mother passed away in 1995, she left seventy-four grandchildren and many more great-grandchildren."

Sister Mary Jane prefers not to tell you how old she is. "My age does not make any difference in what I do and how I live. Wisdom comes with aging," she says with a friendly smile.

The next to the oldest child in a Kentucky Farm Bureau family, Mary Jane was the only one to enter a religious order. The little girl, who once played in a clay pit by the side of her home, grew up to become an artist as well as a nun. After she completed her vows she went out into different school areas to teach art–western, eastern, and northern Kentucky. She served in Ohio, Louisiana, and Arizona before returning to Kentucky to care for her elderly parents.

"When I was studying in Arizona, one of my graduate school professors made a profound impression on me," she says. "There were over a hundred students including military personnel in the class and the professor asked us for our first and last names only. He wanted no titles.

"It freed me up to be who I am. I have become a free, intense, and sensitive individual," she says gently.

Now, surrounded by canvas and clay artwork, Sister Mary Jane is sharing who she is with those who are fortunate enough to sit and chat and learn from her. "I'm just so pleased to have such a beautiful studio to work in," she smiles as she sweeps her hand toward the lovely windows.

The artwork is by the sister and her students–baskets of bright golden zinnias, landscapes of trees in autumnal colors, splashy red tulips–and her clay pots are fanciful and whimsical. "This one is the color of the natural clay," she points to a deep, rich red pot we'd like to take home.

Her students' ages are varied. Some are local residents and some are nuns who reside at Nazareth. Whenever someone says that they want to paint but don't know how, Sister Mary Jane just says, "You come along and I'll show you how. I have students who come in at different times of the day. My emphasis is on motivation–trying to get their thoughts to run in a certain direction."

As for her own works, she feels more comfortable with painting with oils. "I stay away from watercolor," she laughs. "My favorite type of subject is gleaned from nature, natural surroundings."

And, as natural as could be, she says, "I have no problem drawing nudes. I've always had the utmost dignity and reverence for the human body. I've got some nudes over there," she gestures toward a stash of paintings in the corner of her studio.

Sister Mary Jane balances her life as a teacher with her life as a nun whose calling also includes morning and evening prayer and a service of mass during the day. The mission, as stated on the seal of the Sisters of Charity of Nazareth, Kentucky, states, "The love of Christ impels us." Along with her vows of chastity, poverty, and obedience, Sister Mary Jane is also impelled to practice a timeless value she learned from her parents: service to others.

*Lalie*

# RYAN

*R*yan's a "home school" student.

He's fourteen years old (when this was first written in May of 1996), exceptionally bright, takes to algebra the way a duck does to water, is athletic and extroverted (if mountain bike riding is a sign of being more "out" than "in."). He's neither Huck Finn nor Tom Sawyer, but Ryan Haynes of Danville is a living example of Mark Twain's credo: "I never let my schoolin' interfere with my education."

Ryan and his mother, Beverly, a sensitive and thoughtful, professionally driven and committed woman, see positive outcomes resulting from their home school experience. "It's more efficient," says Ryan, who's been staying home and studying for the past three years. "I pretty much teach myself."

"Don't you miss your friends at school?" has been a predictable and frequent question.

"Friends don't really mean much at all. I have one or two true friends [out of about fifteen]. All other people don't hurt for you, so they shouldn't be able to make decisions for you. It's mind games; kids are really mean to kids," says Ryan when asked to share his feelings about peer pressure, especially during the difficult and vulnerable middle school years. And then there's the yellow school bus with the flashing red lights before sunrise. Remembering an acquaintance who rides on the school bus for an hour each day, Ryan shakes his head sympathetically when reminded that some students stay on the bus for at least twice that long. Ryan sleeps an extra hour in the morning and usually finishes his "homework" shortly after midday. He's one of over 6,200 home school students in the Commonwealth of Kentucky, a growing phenomenon but one that's obviously not for everybody. Studying at home requires special motivation, commitment, and disciplined individualism.

Beverly Haynes, a businesswoman who understands both efficiency and quality learning opportunities, pushes her son to go well beyond institutionalized expectations, but she supports Ryan's decision to go next year to a private high school. The only catch: it will probably be a religious school (the Hayneses are Lutheran) and in any event it must have high academic standards.

"It would be easier at school," says ninth-grader Ryan, already well established in two tenth grade courses.

"What grades do you expect to make?"

"A's."

To some it sounds too simple, too neat, too isolated (maybe too elitist, even unpatriotic). Many teachers and administrators in public and private schools believe the give-and-take of peer relationships in and out of the classroom is important preparation for life (sometimes called "The Real World").

"At some point, they're going to have to learn to deal with all kinds of personalities," says one public school teacher, a view that very well may be shared by many educators. While usually seen in a negative light, peer pressure is a challenging element in a broadly based learning environment. Beverly Haynes and her husband combine high-pressured professional careers with the supervision of their son's education. Ryan frequently travels with them, visiting museums, attending educational events, and meeting a variety of people. Ryan and his mother use commuting time to listen to special learning tapes and each other's music preferences.

As she leans against a doorframe at her place of business, Beverly Haynes gives three main considerations for anyone contemplating home school. "The child has to be willing, there must be a commitment, and there must be a lot of give-and-take between the parent and the child."

Ryan does not expect his parents to stand over him, does not need constant supervision. "I have had control of my studies, it's been my thing. I've set up my own schedule," says Ryan with a confident smile.

"But won't you miss the eighth grade prom?"

"You mean they have one?"

"Yes, but not many seem to be interested in dancing. It's mainly noise and standing or running in circles."

"That's kind of silly," laughed Ryan.

"Back to the peer pressure and your opinion of it."

"When I'm with kids who all want to do something, if I think it's wrong, I just tell them I'm not going to do it. If they make fun of me because of that, I just don't care. I'm going to do what I think is right."

Each week, Ryan takes a test in all the courses he studies. He uses approved educational materials, which include test banks. His mother monitors the tests and submits them for scoring. His father's presence is definitely felt. "Dad is in my face every day, taking privileges away (if necessary)...His lectures are the worst."

Ryan, in addition to his mountain biking, is active in Boy Scouts and likes neighborhood basketball and has a goal at age fourteen: "The freedom to do what I want to do."

*Lalie*

# BETTY JO AND JOE

*S*he drives bus Number One. He drives bus Number Five.

Betty Jo is in her thirtieth year behind the wheel of a ten-ton yellow monster of a school bus. Joe is in his twenty-fifth year. They've celebrated their forty-second wedding anniversary.

Let's put a Number Two yellow pencil to the bus-driving part of it:
- they've driven a combined total of fifty-five years
- multiply that times 175 regular school days in a year
- multiply that times the approximate number of total miles they drive each of those days–266
- sixty-one-year-old Betty Jo and seventy-one-year-old Joe Turner have driven approximately 2,560,250 miles over some Bourbon County roads barely wide enough for two small cars to pass.

Betty Jo and Joe Turner have driven the distance between Bangkok and Berlin 478 times. Come to think of it, they've driven to the moon and back five times with miles left over. Altogether, the thirty-four Bourbon County school buses travel the equivalent of a one-way trip to California every day. Those are straight-line miles. The Turners' routes are about as straight as a bowl of spaghetti. Add about fifty children ranging from kindergartners to high school seniors in an average load and that makes for an interesting dish of meatballs.

"You've got to like children," says a smiling, laughing Betty Jo, whose father was also a Kentucky school bus driver. "Daddy had a folding chair beside him...I used to sit in it...Uncle Russell had a school bus...drivers had to buy their own buses in the old days."

Normally stoic Joe speaks up: "I sat up there in the folding chair before she did because my legs were too long." Joe grew up to become a certified instructor for new bus drivers.

"When school gets out, in a couple of weeks I'm ready to get back," says Betty Jo, who quit once: "I said, Joe, I gotta get back on that bus...if there's a job available I want it."

"I love it," says Betty Jo, who gets up at 4:45 every morning. She and Joe have to go out and kick the tires, inspect the air brakes and the lights and all the other safety checks and make sure that "everything under the hood is working all right." (Buses are required to be serviced every thirty days by professional mechanics.)

Two things for parents to tell their children who ride school buses:
• tell them to stay in their seats
• tell them to stay in their seats
Any other Betty Jo Commandments?
• No filthy talk
• No cursing of any kind
• No smoking
• No dipping
• No weapons (that includes pocketknives)

As for the "boy-girl thing": can't slump down in the seats, have to be able to see 'em," says Betty Jo, who has greater fears: "...an eighteen-wheeler coming at you...ice...snow...flash floods."

Throughout the Commonwealth, superintendents are out on the roads at 4 a.m., and it's their go/no-go decision that's final, although all the drivers listen to radios both at home and in the buses. Still, there can be problems, such as ice forming after the children are in school. Betty Jo says that's put "handprints on the steering wheel!" She and all the other drivers are required to attend CPR and first aid classes. Biggest fear of all: a group of children getting off the bus and one of them darting across the road: "I tell them, 'Look at me before crossing...if I'm smiling and nodding "Yes," it's O.K.'"

Are kids the same today as they used to be?

"[Many] kids today don't have respect for anybody with authority, not even themselves. They'll call you everything. They'll say, 'You don't tell me what to do.' They'll use language they hear on television. There's a different parent relationship. Parents have to work, where thirty years ago they didn't. Some children are baby-sitting themselves. Some are left at empty houses. [Kindergarteners and preschoolers are not permitted to be left at a bus stop without someone being there to meet them.] I have parents who won't cooperate. The first time [there's trouble] we talk to the student;

the second time the school officials bring in the parents; the third time we have to take them off the bus.

"I can get awful mad. I can scream and yell," says Betty Jo, while her husband, Joe, looks as silent as a six-foot two-inch rock–you know he's there without him having to say anything.

Betty Jo and Joe have worn out three buses each, and the present Number One and Number Five have a combined mileage of 320,000 miles. As for when these drivers might wear out, Betty Jo says she'll keep on going "as long as I can pass the physical. Every year I say it's going to be my last...[but]...I enjoy it. Don't know what else I'd do."

Joe, he smiles as if he feels pretty much the same way.

*A bus note:* Since this was written Betty Jo and Joe have retired. She drove her bus for thirty-two years, he drove his for twenty-five. They've celebrated their 44th wedding anniversary. On Betty Jo's last day, David and I made a sentimental journey to school. David reached up to the window on the steering wheel side and shook the driver's hand. I posed for a picture. Our daughter, Ravy Bradford Dick, rode home to Plum Lick for the last time with Betty Jo.

*Lalie*

# NOGGIN POWER

*A*pril Fools' Day has put me up on my soapbox to orate about such an ill-advised idea as believing we're bamboozled only once a year, get it out of our system, and rise above all numskulled, featherbrained, mooncalfed notions the other 364 days.

Consider the possibility of not being able to find enough good people to do hard work. Edna Ferber's *So Big* is a brilliant description of tireless truck farmers supplying fresh vegetables to a hungry Chicago. Edna Ferber is a fine example of an accomplished novelist too poor to go to college.

Think about the likelihood that a valedictorian or salutatorian doesn't have enough accumulated knowledge to know the difference between pickled chopped cabbage and sauerkraut. Happens.

Grade inflation happens. Everything else is inflated–egos, estimations, the price of a candy bar–so why not raise "E" to "D," "D" to "C," "C" to "B," and "B" to "A?" Come to think of it, why not give everybody an "A" and stop worrying about it? That way all of us will feel good because we're excellent no matter how big (or rotten) the cabbage is.

We wouldn't have to learn anything. We could just write a check for, say, 120 "A's" over a four-year period and not have to spend any money on books. We'd have more for candy bars and other good stuff.

Janice Holt Giles didn't go to college because she was too busy writing *Hannah Fowler, The Kentuckians*, and *The Believers*. Imagine what might have happened if she'd been on the education fast track! She might have gotten a mention in the *Encyclopedia of Literature*.

There is one Giles in this reference volume: *Giles Goat-Boy; or The Revised New Syllabus*. Might want to go there sometime. Might want to help write a new study guide, a new roadmap for Kentucky. Want to come along?

Here's some food for thought, an All Fools' Day question for a classroom full of students hungry for the truth about sauerkraut: "Do we know where we're going?"

These late winter-early spring ideas are not intended to trash the idea of college or any other formal education. Nor is it to say that a high school diploma or a college degree is necessarily bogus or a certain waste of time. It is to say that high school and college can be enriching, but they're no guarantee for a fulfilling life, not even a predictable career.

Avoiding college won't automatically turn us into a Ferber or a Giles. Staying away from a trade school won't willy-nilly make us an electrician or a plumber or a welder.

We have these things called brains. They work best when they're free. Good thinking produces good actions. Marvelous noggins on top of our shoulder blades, cabbage or a mess of sauerkraut, they're capable of grander outcomes. It has been said that we use a fraction of our brainpower. Who convinced us that that was a good hill of potatoes?

A new millennial idea might be a combination of many thingamajigs: decency, sensitivity, diligence, fairness, courage, commitment, persistence, and spirituality. Make up your own list. Take one of the generalizations and fill it in with your own specifics.

A few discards we might want to shed in the last year of the old century roaring out in glory (or a resounding thud?): something for nothing, minimum effort for maximum reward, instant gratification, Billy Bockfusses who can't tell one goat from another.

Who in the name of all creation was Billy Bockfuss? A character in John Barth's satirical novel, he represents a challenge to read more about the university that symbolizes the world. The university should not be apart from the rest of us. And those who don't attend should not be apart from it.

We all have an important piece of the grand puzzle. What we do as individuals will move the community toward a wiser century. Maybe.

We'll probably continue the custom of All Fools' Days, and we'll be fortunate if it happens only once a year.

*David*

# MORE NOGGIN POWER

From time to time, a reader writes to question something I've written. That's fine, because it helps to know there's somebody out there.

I've decided not to use names because it might discourage her/him from writing again.

The words in question were the ones for All Fools' Day this past April. The headline writer called it "Noggin Power."

The third paragraph included the following: "Think about the likelihood that a valedictorian or salutatorian doesn't have enough accumulated knowledge to know the difference between pickled chopped cabbage and sauerkraut."

At the top of the story, Jackie Larkins's illustration showed a jar of "sauerkraut" and a jar and plateful of "pickled chopped cabbage."

The reader's letter included the following: "I must confess that I don't know the difference between pickled chopped cabbage and sauerkraut, further I have asked over twenty people today and none knew the difference. I have a call in to our extension home economist, hoping she can tell me. It appears we have a serious shortage of 'Noggin' power down here."

Nay, nay, there's plenty of good thinking in every direction. It may be a case of occasional, honest, well-meaning, misfired communication. It may be a metaphor that has not succeeded as well as the author had intended. As John B. Opdycke has written in his *Mark My Words,*: "Metaphor implies the similarity between one object and another usually unlike, by speaking of the one as if it were the other and omitting all signs of the comparison made."

O.K. A head of cabbage is a metaphor for the cranium containing brains. Whether what passes for brains is sauerkraut or pickled chopped cabbage is an individual matter. The important issue is whether thinking is occurring, however imperfect it may be.

In her Pulitzer Prize winning novel, *So Big*, Edna Ferber, although she never went to college, indicated she knew quite a lot about cabbages and kings and children and parents who have their priorities mixed, if not their metaphors. Her main character, Selina, knew her way in and about many kinds of vegetables of the soil, knew her beans as well as her cabbages.

The *American Heritage Dic-tion-ary of the English Language, Third Edition*, defines "sauerkraut" as "chopped or shredded cabbage salted and fermented in its own juice." The difference between "fermented" and "pickled" is a narrow one; therefore, if anybody wants to challenge the metaphor with the technical difference, it helps to prove that there's room for rhubarb.

The difference between "pickled chopped cabbage and sauerkraut" might be in the mind of the beholder. To some it has to do with pH, acidity, and microbes. To me it has something to do with discernment, curiosity, and the notion that a mind is a repository where growth is possible and wisdom is not something that can be foolproof on a grocery shelf. Possibly putting it this way would have strengthened the metaphor: "The similarity of pickled chopped cabbage, sauerkraut, and the human brain."

"Pickled chopped cabbage" is obviously at the root of the hotbed of controversy, however some might find interesting the word history of "pickle" on page 1369 of *The American Heritage*: "It [pickle] was applied, as it had been in Middle Dutch, to a pickling solution. Later pickle was used to refer to something so treated, such as a cucumber. The word also took on a figurative sense, 'a troublesome situation,' perhaps under the influence of a similar Dutch usage in the phrase in de pickel zitten, 'sit in the pickle.'"

Rather than describe my usage as "poor," I would suggest a certain "plentifulness" of harvested thought whose intent was to stimulate new considerations concerning the quality and the mission of public education.

It seems to me that when schools inflate grades, and students are unwilling to be considered as anything less than "excellent," there's a fermenting possibility that we may be "sitting in the pickle" and not realize it until we're stewed in our own juice.

So, three cheers for "noggin power" and keep those cards and letters coming!

*David*

# BELT-TIGHTENING

*I*n 1991 we were cutting the budget at the School of Journalism at the University of Kentucky. It hurt. We knew we were going to have to make fewer professional trips and fewer long distance telephone calls. We would publish fewer newsletters, cut back on subscriptions to publications, postpone the hiring of additional talented and committed faculty, delay the replacement of outdated equipment, conduct new fundraising campaigns, and accept more unraked leaves and unbuffed hallways.

Most of us were ready to increase our efforts to serve our students. Even if we had to meet them outside under trees or deep inside damp caves, we would do it. Fortunately, that's not the kind of world in which we live, nor the kind of marketplace where graduates will be seeking careers.

Maxine Paetro, author of *How to Put Your Book Together and Get a Job in Advertising*, spoke on the Lexington campus. She told students, "I'm looking for the best of the best...bright young people to move us into the future."

What is true for advertising in the UK School of Journalism is also true for newspaper, radio, and television newsgatherers, public relations professionals, and journalism educators. What is true for the UK College of Communications is true for every other college on the Lexington campus and throughout the Commonwealth. Each dollar removed from the budget of higher education is a dollar unspent to prepare students to assume leadership roles in the new century.

In an age of advanced communications technology and theory, it becomes a puzzlement why there's been no better explanation as to how the budget "shortfall" occurred. The easy answer was the recession spreading across the nation. It was expected to continue into 1992. That may have been the headline, but other possibilities might have included: a general weariness growing out of boredom; frustration with a culture too often appearing to reward villains; a civilization that also seemed to have lost touch with values of decency, fairness, and cooperativeness.

In the spirit of the latter, the faculty of the UK School of Journalism was willing to cut what already was a modest budget. That alone would not improve the situation. In order to provide the nation with "...the best of the best...bright young people to move us into the future," it was necessary for each member of the faculty to rededicate her- or himself to more and better quality teaching. There would need to be more and better quality research and public service.

If the rest of society, especially public officials in Frankfort, will take a similar view, then we may stand a chance of turning the hurt we feel into the help we need. One of the benefits of budget cutting is that those involved are brought together to sit at a table where the focus is more intense and sustained than in normal situations. The reality is that we need to be spending more, not less, on higher education. The Commonwealth should expect the best of the best. Otherwise, college will become bicycle wheels with fewer spokes–students will find the riding wobbly.

One danger at budget-cutting time is the possibility that too many Kentuckians view higher education as a luxury item. In an advanced civilization it is fundamental. The Commonwealth can't compete in a global market if students are ill-served by a bare-bones curriculum taught by professors who must spend less when more is clearly needed.

Many of us in higher education will accept the cuts as unavoidable belt-tightening. We'll bear our share, and we'll work harder than ever to make sure as many of our students as possible have a chance to become "the best."

But there are limits to forbearance. Lord preserve us when all the good teachers abandon ship.

*David*

# CHEATING 101

*A*s soon as I heard about a new best-selling book, *Cheating 101*, I decided it was time for action. This "won't stand," as President Bush liked to say.

To make matters worse, the book was written by a journalism student, Michael Moore, of Rutgers University. Journalists have enough bad baggage without one of their prospective own engaging in this kind of—well, what's the best word for it? Baggage or garbage? Take your pick.

The way I understand it, Mr. Moore believes a lot of the problem is due to the teachers. What's that? Sure, according to the report I read in a recent (1992) *Boston Globe* story reprinted in the *Lexington Herald-Leader*, it's those teachers again, those ill-prepared teachers, those professors "not interested in what they're doing....It's a manual about their mistakes, their shortcomings, and failures."

O.K., now I get it. The teachers are responsible for the fact that students are driven to cheat like ducks to water. Of course, the author is said to believe that one should not cheat in the major or in nonrequired courses where they really do want to learn something. But all the rest of that "stuff"– why, cheat your heart away.

I taught Journalism 101 at the University of Kentucky, and I didn't believe in cheating in that or any other course. Who's kidding whom? Anybody who cheats her or his way through to a degree has nobody to blame but the cheater when it comes time to sort out the real folks from the bogus folks in the job market.

After I read about *Cheating 101*, I told my students in Journalism 101 that it was causing me to add a little something extra on the midterm and the final examinations. Even with well over 115 to 150 students in the class, where multiple choice questions become almost a practical necessity, I decided to add some essay questions. Mr. Moore may have a method for cheating on an assortment of essay questions, but I seriously doubt that it'll work.

It isn't fun playing traffic cop when students resort to all kinds of cheating. I hated it then and I hate it now. If anybody thought I'd let *Cheating 101* go unchallenged, they had another think coming. Yep–some will still cheat in spite of everything, and they'll miss the essential point: cheat is another word for impostor, fraud, quack.

Even if it were true that it's largely the fault of ill-prepared, uninspired, and uninspiring teachers, cheating would not be the answer. I've always believed a good student can overcome a bad teacher any day in the week. But rationalizing cheating as the way to do it is insulting at best.

If somebody is not ready to go to college to learn without cheating, that somebody ought to dig ditches for a while. They could practice their cheating there. Or they could take up skydiving and practice cheating there.

I'm riled, and I know it. But I can't help it. This whole thing about academic cheating is sad. When we become a nation of cheaters we do a disservice to everybody–but especially to ourselves.

Mr. Moore has every right to make money out of his book. The First Amendment has him covered. But the only way he can succeed is if a lot of people buy what he's selling. If there weren't a market he wouldn't be doing it.

What I'd like to see is a nation of students who will look cheating squarely in the eye and say: "It's not for me...I've better things to do."

*David*

213

# FLIGHT INSTRUCTIONS

*T*he end of another spring semester on college campuses has brought more students to the realization that it's time to test wings. Flapping feathers on the edge of the academic nest bears little resemblance to the summer's work. For seniors it means that after summer comes fall, and for many, a cold and uncertain winter.

Some tips from an old pilot who has been through his share of stormy weather:

- Don't see how high you can fly and by all means leave stunting to the jocks who've nothing much better to do
- Try to depart and arrive on time
- Concentrate on where you're going; aimlessly soaring may seem like a fun thing to do, but the fare-paying passengers will probably find simple, sane, and safe trips more to their liking
- Be nice to your passengers; many of them are responsible for you having a plane with a cockpit complete with navigational instruments
- Smile even when it hurts; a frowning pilot isn't the best confidence builder
- Stay awake
- Rest up between trips
- Don't drink and fly
- Try to save fuel
- Know your co-pilot; knowing your navigator is also good business; it's hard to imagine doing and saying silly things that have the remotest potential to spook either your co-pilot or your navigator; it's like teamwork on the highest trapeze (without a net)

- Pay attention to detail, especially baggage; passengers are particular about these little things, and if you can love their baggage they'll probably love you.

Most of these tips are not taught in college, possibly because they're considered too obvious. Hardly anything could be farther from the truth. The most educated flyer in the world who does not understand the basics is an aviator who may wind up folding paper planes and bouncing them off walls.

A college education is a fine thing to have. But if it's not underwritten with fundamental street smarts, disasters loom in every corner of the sky. These days, good flying jobs are hard enough to find and keep. It's probably also well to remember that not all the "best" jobs are in the pilot's seat. There's much to be done on the ground, in the control tower, at the corporate office, at the ticket counters, and out along the curbside.

Teamwork means working cooperatively toward a common goal. The Commonwealth of Kentucky might well be called the Commongoal of Kentucky. Goals need not be simplistic. They can and should be richly complex. It's when we don't listen well to those trying to communicate with us that we have close calls, or worse yet–midair collisions.

There's plenty of room in the sky, but the allocations are limited and there's always the danger of disaster. There are no guarantees, no failsafe, no giant net to catch those upon whom fate has frowned a final time. But despite the uncertainties, it's worth it to be out there testing the wind currents.

*David*

# NANCY

*N*ancy Sherburne's memorial service was on a stage, where it should have been. At the end of the service there was a standing ovation, as there should have been.

Nancy was more than Nancy.

She was Mary Todd Lincoln, "one of the best educated women of her era." She was Laura Clay, "nationally known advocate for women's right to vote." And yes, she was Belle Breezing, "a famous Lexington bawd who ran the most orderly of disorderly houses."

Nancy Sherburne was a Chautauqua character, making it possible for others to look back through a peephole of time where names and places might otherwise remain brittle on yellowing pages of historical writing.

Born in Iowa, she and her Michigan-born husband, Jim, made Kentucky their home. With their presence they breathed more life into it, Nancy as an actress and a Chautauqua character for the Kentucky Humanities Council, Jim as a novelist, his books including *Rivers Run Together* and *Death's Bright Arrow*.

There were no prayers offered aloud for Nancy on the beautiful fall afternoon on the campus of Midway College where she and Jim had taught drama and English literature. There was no great choir singing, only the sound of birds through the chapel's open window. There was no mighty organ playing, only the sliver of an old friend's voice singing "I Walk Through the Garden" and the sureness of a guitarist playing. Nancy's last audience softly whispered the idea that you've got to go by yourself through "this lonely valley" to come out together on the other side.

Friends and family came forward, walked up the aisle, one by one took their places stage center. They stood amid the pictures–Nancy and Jim on their honeymoon in Greenwich Village–and the flowers. These walk-ons provided other peepholes to the old and the recent days with Nancy Sherburne.

One of the last times I'd seen her was at Bill Nave's annual Derby party (he preceded Nancy to the other side by one month almost to the day). We talked about Belle Breezing, Lexington's notorious madam from about 1876 to 1917, Nancy's favorite Chautauqua character, according to husband Jim. We chose to view Belle in terms of hypocrisy.

After all, who were all the males who made Belle's house so infamous? Why did only she and her employees deserve to wear scarlet? Nancy and I were not prepared to throw first stones.

Near the end of Nancy Sherburne's memorial service, husband Jim rose and took his place upon the stage. He read a story about "having it here, right here, in the heart" and each time he said the word he placed his hand upon his breast. He didn't cry, not at this moment he didn't outwardly weep. Once, before the services began, he'd looked out the window at the giant tree shedding its leaves. He knew a certain time had come. He'd not written *Death's Clenched Fist* for nothing.

A young woman who had been a student of Nancy's at Midway College came forward and with her superb guitar she played and sang "My Old Kentucky Home." I had never before heard it so well done. Surely Nancy would have approved.

Walking back across the campus of the school founded in 1847, I thought about what might be left of the rest of my own life–more importantly, what lay ahead in the new millennium for the Commonwealth of Kentucky. Reminding myself to continue to beware of absolutes and oversimplifications, I imagined that Nancy Sherburne was saying from her new vantage point, Don't take yourself quite so seriously. Reach down inside your self of selves and bring forth the best that is there. Resist the temptation to be judgmental.

The core, the essence of Nancy, as I see it now, was explained by one of her friends up there on the stage of life. Know who you are, and be who you are, and be comfortable with that, whether you're a Mary Todd Lincoln, a Laura Clay, or a Belle Breezing.

The madam shouldn't be included with the other two ladies? Possibly not. But who knows what was beautiful in any of their hearts?

*David*

217

# BIG RED

$O$nce every century or so there's a horse that so captures the imagination of humans it transcends superlatives. You stand there in the animal's presence and you feel supremacy of beauty and power. You sense atypical intelligence, and the normal distance between humanity and equine animal has narrowed to such a closeness that the bonding is breathtaking.

Secretariat.

He was Byron's noble steed.

The name alone, instantly recognizable, always memorable, was as magnificent as Man O' War. When anyone spoke the name, Secretariat, you knew what it meant. It was certainly not the office of a governmental department. Secretariat brought back thrilling memories of the amazing, records-smashing Triple Crown victories of 1973, especially the Belmont Stakes win by thirty-one lengths.

Secretariat was hands down Bourbon County's best known citizen. Tourists by the tens of thousands made their pilgrimages to Claiborne Farm on the edge of Paris to see the champion, the wonder horse, and their idol. It is difficult to describe the setting, the landscape across which Secretariat moved with such authority and grace. He had style and class, and he knew it. He had the poise that comes with good breeding. He had the assurance that makes unnecessary a show of boldness. Yet he also possessed the ability to be playful when the mood struck him.

Life for Secretariat was more than finishing thirty-one lengths ahead of all the other horses that ran in the 1973 Belmont Stakes. It was more than the over five hundred matings of his stud career. Life for Secretariat included unusual, instinctive behavior that caused him to understand humanity's need for something special and exceptional.

A man or a woman without a horse, especially a fine horse, is an incomplete man or woman. Richard III would have given his kingdom for a horse, but beyond a need born of desperation there's an enriching necessity that only comes with a Secretariat–a sweet, powerful excellence unobtainable by humans. Herein lies the mystery. It embraces the unique relationship mankind shares with dogs, and dogs with horses too. There's a cross-species kinship, a bonding that improves our humanity in a way otherwise unobtainable.

Secretariat may have been syndicated for more than $6 million, but no value could be placed on the way he looked at those who came to look at him. His instinctive intelligence included the ability to know that his influence crossed the usual boundaries of the world of horses. He walked into the hearts and minds of men, women, and children. He stayed for a while, then romped back across his paddock to be just a famous horse again.

Secretariat needed man; man needed Secretariat. Neither would be finished without the other. Perhaps it speaks to the universality of all God's creatures. We are dependent. No longer should we think of even remote or exotic subspecies as nondependent. Each one of us is endangered and the endangerment is complex.

Without a Secretariat to make our spirits soar we become increasingly earthbound. Without a Secretariat to put a smile on our face, a tingle throughout our being, we become joyless. Other means are available– children, an autumn sun slanting through the changing colors of the leaves, a squirrel scampering across a high wire on a city street, spiders on frosty mornings spinning their webs up and down the October countryside. Yet without the horse the specter of the incomplete human being still haunts us.

As the days of 1989 wind down, and the leaves of another October turn yellow and red and fall to the ground, the horse cemetery at Claiborne encompasses the body of Secretariat. His fans will visit there in the seasons ahead, and yet the memory of the great Triple Crown stallion will still be living back at the stable, in the jockey rooms of the land, and down on the rail of every racetrack across the nation.

Secretariat was the kind of horse by which other thoroughbreds measure greatness.

*David*

219

# LITTLE ICE MAN

*"If I had a donkey wot wouldn't go, d'ya think I'd wollop him?*
*No, no, no."*

Jacob Beuler and Charles Dickens

*I* never knew miniature donkeys almost always have a cross to bear. I never knew there was such a thing as miniature donkeys until I visited Glen and Frieda at their Vanoy's Lazy Acres farm in Casey County.

They showed me how Mother Nature has drawn one long line from the donkey's head to its tail, a shorter line from one shoulder across to the other, making a perfect cross. It's almost as if the Great Designer decided, "There's just one more little thing I want to add to one of the smallest of my creatures."

When Frieda retired after forty-five years of teaching, she told her husband, Glen, she'd like to take on a new hobby. They decided it would be miniature donkeys. Now they've got so many funny, cuddly little critters on their four-hundred-acre farm, they're thinking enough may be enough, already.

And then there're llamas, geese, two black swans, six pigmy goats, beef cattle, dogs, and cats galore on what was supposed to be Vanoy's Lazy Acres Farm. You have to listen closely to absorb Frieda's commentary as she walks through the donkey nursery. "Now that's Darlene, daughter of Carmella, which was Glen's favorite donkey, and that's Darlene's daughter, Daisy. Meggie is the daughter of Margaret, and Buford pulled the little cart in the Kentucky Derby parade. Buford is the grey jack, Patrick is the grey-brown jack, B.J. is the [are you ready for this?] black jack, and Little Ice Man is the solid white albino, blue-eyed jack, and hello, little babies, how are you today?"

Four miniature donkey jacks and fifty jennies later, Glen and Frieda have a right to believe they've got more than their share of crosses to bear. "You can get attached, can't hardly let them go, babies grow up [to become] mamas and grandmamas," says Frieda.

But they will have to let them go, and they do–for a price. But before anybody decides to pay $500 for a little weanling jack, or $2,500 to $3,000 for a pregnant jenny (depending on color and conformation), or $3,000 for a mature jack, they'll have to come to terms with one fact. This is one nativity scene that can't be boxed and stored in the attic after Christmas.

The bray goes on. So does the hay bill. So does the corn bill. So do the apples and carrots bills. So do the costs of the visits of the farrier to trim feet. So do the vet bills.

After making these real-world calculations, here are some more guides to happy times with miniature donkeys. They can't be over thirty-six inches tall, ground to shoulder. (The small standard-size donkey is from 36.01 to 40 inches tall. Next comes the standard, from 40.01 to 48, and finally there's the large standard, 48 to 54 inches.)

Some publications to read if ever the miniature donkey idea hee-haws in your mind: there're *Miniature Donkey Talk* (the talk of all the world), published in Westminster, Maryland, and *Asset*, published by the National Miniature Donkey Association of Rome, New York.

Here are some frequently asked questions about miniature donkeys.

Do they kick? Usually only other donkeys when they get into an argument over who's going to stand where at the eating place.

Do they bite? Usually only other donkeys when the mood seems right for it.

Are they adorable? No question about it, they win the adorable prize.

Are they gentle? No question about it, they win the gentle prize.

Are they easy to care for? Depends on how many miniature donkeys you're talking about.

Diminishing returns apply to miniature donkeys too.

Are they available for nativity scenes? They've been known to show up at churches in Casey County–but guess what? Each night, Glen and Frieda feel a responsibility to take them home.

Although miniature donkeys are able to pull carts, and the Bufords and the Darlenes and the Little Ice Men can bear the weight of children, these creatures with the unusual mark of the cross on their backs can bear only so much. Just like human beings, they have a need for love. They're vulnerable. They shouldn't be taken for granted. After the holidays, they shouldn't be forgotten until December rolls in again.

*David*

# COST OF UNDERSTANDING

"Do you still believe in Santa Claus?" asked the older child, ominously.

"Yes," the younger child said shyly, as if being asked, "Do you still believe the sun will rise in the morning?"

"David b'lieves in Santa Claus, David b'lieves in Santa Claus," chanted the older child.

My face felt vaguely uncomfortable. This question about Santa Claus had been peeping over the limitations of my impressionable mind for a year or more. There had been so many confusing Santas in movies (before there was television), so many ragtag department store Santas, not to mention those who popped, like a bad cold, in and out of schools and churches. The problem was the idea that even if (God forbid) there was no Santa Claus, there should have been one and there should always be one.

There were whispers, side-glances, knowing smiles during this time when I was troubled by the possibility of there being no Santa Claus. The feeling was like a numbness on some days, on other days it was more like an older boy's fist in the pit of my stomach. At those times, the breath went out of me and the fear that took its place seemed unbearable. Figuring it out, though, required too much thinking. It was more comfortable to enjoy the feeling of Santa. How such a fat fellow managed to squeeze down a small chimney, especially one with a hot fire in it, was Santa's problem. He could figure it out.

The part about Mrs. Claus and the helpers had a sweetness about it that charmed the socks off me. Everybody in Santa's workshop seemed to enjoy life the way it should be enjoyed–without a care in the world. They reminded me of the Seven Dwarfs. I loved Snow White, and I was jealous of any princes prancing to and fro in the forest. They were no different from the Big Bad Wolf, who didn't seem to know how to keep his hands off Red

Riding Hood. The fact that Wolf wanted to feast on Grandma was another matter; it was beyond my ability to solve such grownup puzzles. Little Jack Horner, who sat in a corner, eating his Christmas pie, was as real as any of the other major players in my little boy's imagination. Who dared say there was no Jack Horner who stuck in his thumb and pulled out a plum and said, "What a good boy am I?"

But of all the wonderful fairyland folk, Santa led the way.

"C'm'ere, let me show you something," said the older boy, leading me to the living room closet. He opened the door. There were the presents, the ones Santa should have been bringing in a few hours. The older boy had the decency not to say, "There's your Santa Claus," but even if he had, it wouldn't have made any difference. In that one flashing moment I gained something, and I lost something. I gained a piece of understanding. I lost a piece of magic.

We closed the door and turned away.

The days of my life moved forward on the memories of Christmases past.

*David*

# CHRISTMAS GETS THE BUSINESS

"Christmas Gets the Business" was a rejected television documentary title I tried to persuade WHAS-TV to air about twenty-five years ago (thirty-eight years ago in 1999, but nothing much has changed). I suppose it was felt that the title was a tad too impudent to suit the sales department, which never wanted to give the slightest offense to the station's advertisers, who never wanted to offer the slightest discouragement to the customers, who might shell out their cash for the latest gimcrack or two.

Near the end of the twentieth century I'm just as convinced that Christmas does get the business. The best part of my crudely but sincerely done one-man documentary was the name of it, and if anybody wanted to kill the double-edged message, the quickest way was to meat ax the title.

Christmas business isn't likely to go away in our lifetimes or our children's children's lifetimes. (Authors too rejoice that books sell better at Christmas.) In our culture, Christmas barter is as natural as bees building honeycombs. And that's the way it is until something intrudes with awesome power and hellish determination as if to declare, "You damn well better know that Christmas is getting the business." Moreover, it could be high time that some of us start to give Christmas as much undivided attention as we're now giving the business of Christmas.

Sometimes the earth has to move before we're aware that there's a power greater than our poor, feeble, man-made efforts to construct every December 25 to suit ourselves, whiskers and all.

*Terremoto* is the Spanish word for earthquake, and the literal meaning is "earth moved." It was a little before midnight on the eve of Christmas Eve, in 1972, when the word "*Terremoto!*" was heard like a collective, mighty gasp through the capital city of Managua, Nicaragua. In those frightful moments when the earth moved, people who had been preparing for another

225

Christmas as usual were snatched from their beds. They were squeezed among the debris of their crumbled houses, swallowed by the convulsing city center. It was as if to notify all that whatever anybody happened to be doing or thinking, it was nothing compared to the universal convulsion of *Terremoto*.

I was in Atlanta at the time, preparing for another Christmas as usual too. The telephone rang and the voice said, "There's been a major earthquake in Managua. We have a Learjet waiting for you at the Atlanta airport."

In all my nineteen years of working for CBS News, I never turned down an assignment. Whenever I received "the call," I went. As Clarence Gibbons, a cameraman from Prattville, Alabama, used to say, "If you're waiting on me, you're dragging your feet." On the way to the Atlanta airport I stopped at a drugstore and bought first aid supplies from the shelf–bandages, surgical dressings, antiseptic solutions, no toys, no candy, no Christmas ties–only those things that might relieve suffering.

On the long ride from Atlanta down to Miami and then across Cuba and the Caribbean to Managua, I put my head back into my folded hands, and I thought deeply about what might be the real meaning of Christmas. I remembered all those early home sweet Kentucky Christmas mornings at Mt. Auburn in Bourbon County, where I'd lived my formative years. I recalled the feeling of innocence, the joy born of small gifts, and the pungent smells of Christmas cooking. I pictured myself sitting on the top step of that antebellum winding staircase, waiting for Jane and Florence and Warren and Billy to join me there because the unspoken rule was: nobody goes down to the Christmas tree until we all do, together. For me, *Terremoto*–if I had known the word–would have meant tearing into simply but wonderfully wrapped packages, and it was racing to the fireplace mantle to take down the long stockings bulging with candy, fruit, and nuts, and maybe a surprise or two. *Terremoto* would be the fireworks we lit each year on the snow-covered front lawn at Mt. Auburn: Roman candles, sparklers, and skyrockets that lit up the peaceful countryside.

The night sky over Managua, Nicaragua, on December 24, 1972, was a dull gray. As I looked from the window of the Learjet there was no sparkling city visible. "Managua, Nicaragua, Is a Wonderful Town" was buried somewhere in memory. Not even the Andrews Sisters could change that now. As we came in from the north over Lake Managua, we searched in the darkness for the slightest appearance of the capital city.

The lights were out–the Christmas lights too. Christmas had definitely gotten the business.

Our pilot banked the Lear in a long slope to the east, and we came in for our landing at the main airport. For a while, everything seemed normal. Maybe the earth had not moved at the airport, and there was a temptation to say aloud, "Where's the damned story?" After we rolled to a stop, we could see that President Somoza's National Guard was dealing as best it could with the sudden influx of unscheduled Christmas Eve arrivals from the United States, those who came in quickly like birds of prey.

An old friend, cameraman Bernie Nudelman, had arrived earlier from Miami, and he knew that the only way to get into the city was to climb onto one of the refugee trucks, any one of the many refugee trucks, and hope for the best. Riding into Managua with the rescue teams left me with a feeling of heartfelt helplessness. All the same, there was the instinctive urge to see, hear, and feel the story, then to tell it to the audience back home in the United States, especially to those wrapping their gifts in Kentucky. I still had my sack of first aid supplies, like a Santa Claus on an unexpected mission of mercy, but there would be no chimneys to climb down in Nicaragua. Even if there had been, *Terremoto* would have bounded to the floor first.

A steady stream of survivors was heading out of the city. Some walked in a daze. Others were jammed into buses and trucks like chickens on their way to processing plants. There was a numbness. An old man mindlessly swept the sidewalk in front of what had been his home. Later in the day, on my way back to the airport, I saw the same old man sitting in a chair on the swept sidewalk as if to tell the world he still had one small piece of earth to call his own. The *hombre viejo* stared vacantly in the direction of the cathedral where the clock was frozen just past midnight–and so it would remain for many days. Why would the cathedral be the object of the wrath of

227

*Terremoto?* One answer is that earthquakes don't have wraths. They are simply earthquakes. Would not the central place of worship be an exception to the universal necessity to reorder earthly structures? Apparently not. I had no easy answers then, nor do I now.

The shocking reality was that *Terremoto* had killed thousands of human beings. First estimates were about 20,000; later it was officially determined to be 5,000. There were possibly 10,000 injuries. I personally delivered first aid supplies to President Somoza as he stood among the emergency field hospital tents. A soft wind played at the edges of the tent flaps; it made the nuns' habits flutter as they walked among the injured.

Why recall the brutal, exceptional past in a book titled *Home Sweet Kentucky?* Just to remind us that the true meaning of Christmas only seems to have so much to do with business. If Christmas "gets the business," business will be left with shallow profit. It took *Terremoto* to convince me that the simpler the Christmas, the better the possibility for the spirit of Christmas. Perhaps we are fated for business-driven Christmases, and maybe it will always be thus–until we have the courage to effect change, before a *Terremoto* does it for us.

*David*

# HENRY YODER

───────────────── ✑ ─────────────────

*H*enry Yoder doesn't speak for all the Mennonites in Fleming County. (He says there may be as many as two hundred in thirty households.) He speaks for himself within a community rich in tradition in the world, but all the while distinctly apart from it.

Henry is twenty-one-years-old. When he looks at you with his soft eyes, the sincerity and depth of his beliefs make their mark on an outsider's consciousness. As he sits in a carpenter's shop near Wallingford just north of the Goddard covered bridge, he's another quiet Kentuckian patiently explaining what it means to be a Mennonite.

"The principle of modesty is the governing principle," he says, his manner exemplifying the thought, his narrow suspenders a symbol of a different attitude about how one should live.

"To be a Mennonite separates us from the mainstream. We do not have television. No radio. We do have the weather radio," Henry adds. "We try to be Christians. We study the Bible. We live the way we feel God wants us to live. We don't follow after churches that are not separated from the world. The people of God must be separate from the world."

Henry's fourteen-year-old brother John and Louie Yoder, co-owner of Wood Craft, builders of gazebos, join us and listen in. They seem interested, but they don't speak unless spoken to. They are respectful of a conversation already started.

"What grade are you in, John?"

"Going into the eighth."

When school begins again, Henry will be his

brother John's science teacher. Henry will use Mennonite textbooks to explain the phenomenon of weather, the realities of temperatures, and other useful stuff like gravity and astronomy. Formal education ends with the eighth grade, but one has the feeling that learning will always continue. Simplicity takes its rightful place alongside modesty.

From a young age, Mennonite children learn the value of work. "If six-, eight-, and ten-year-olds are not taught to work, a prime opportunity is missed. There won't be dedicated perseverance. The American work force is not nearly what it could be," says Henry Yoder, who hastens to add his awareness of child labor laws. "There are plenty of things children can do."

The Wood Craft shop adjoins a cottage industry of bottled honey and preserves. There's a telephone and an adding machine and a fax but no computer. It's a quiet Saturday afternoon and the only things humming are the insects in the gardens. When a rain cloud arrives, John Yoder offers to go out and put the windows up in the outsider's car. He does it quietly, thoughtful in that he sees a need and fills it without hesitation. He remembers to ask first.

"Do you all behave in school?"

John smiles the answer to the question that did not need asking. "We have the right of correction," says the science teacher, the message sent softly but clearly that misbehavior will not be tolerated.

The Mennonites east of Flemingsburg remind their customers that business is not conducted on Sunday. Church is a given, and the assumption is that it's a strict requirement. Religious devotions occur daily in the home, morning, noon, and night. Yet being a Mennonite must be voluntary.

Watching the young Mennonite women working at Yoder's Country Market on KY 32–one sweeping the front porch, another in the kitchen where bread is being baked, another at the cash register, another politely answering customers' questions–an outsider gets the feeling that nobody is forced to do anything. The females cover their heads and wear traditional clothes because they choose to live apart from the world of changing fashion.

"Are there defections?"

"Some. Not many," says Henry Yoder, remembering a friend who has left the discipline but still lives in the area: "We don't cut off all ties."

Well, since there's no television, no radio (other than the weather band), no movies, no taverns in the town, newspapers only now and then, what does Henry Yoder (unmarried) do for entertainment?

He looks through the window to the foothills of the Appalachians and talks of going for walks, "usually three to five miles; a long walk might be fifteen to twenty miles."

Henry is an embodiment of a saying on the wall: "You can't change the past, but you can ruin a perfectly good present by worrying over the future."

It's a forty-mile drive back to Plum Lick, and when I arrive I take out the small loaf of banana nut bread, spread some Yoder blackberry jam on it, and tell my wife, "I think the world would probably be a better place if there were more Mennonites in it."

*David*

# BOBBING FOR EDUCATION?

$\mathcal{I}$t's time once again to vote, and it might be compared to bobbing for apples in a tubful of water that hasn't been changed since the last party. That says as much about the bobbers as it does the bobbed. You'd think enough good people would grow so tired of stale water that they would empty the tub and look for a fresh bunch of apples. The way it usually seems to work, hardly anybody has an appetite for this quadrennial variety of apple until it's a case of being more or less enticed or otherwise bludgeoned with guilt sticks to get down on our knees, put our hands behind our back, and go at it like dodo birds. The more obvious difference between the dodo and us is that the bird is extinct and we are so plentiful.

Down here on Plum Lick we think we're coming to understand that education, just like a good governor, is more than a once-every-four-years apple floating in old political water. A governor of the Commonwealth of Kentucky must be committed to better education for the entire 1,460 days of her or his term in office. The voters must insist on it.

Education is another word for information, knowledge, culture, and mental development–not for the elite or a lucky few, but for as many Kentuckians as possible. There's never been a justification for our low ranking in education when compared with other states. We need strong and inspired leadership, not somebody who will just tell us what we want to hear in order to be elected to the office of governor, a self-serving promise here, another one over there. We need a strong and inspired population of voters willing to set aside slick media blitzes, glib courthouse square proclamations, and old habits of "It was good for Pa and Silas, it's good enough for me."

Shouldn't we be having an honest heart-to-heart talk with our little pea-picking selves? Don't we want a better state for our generations to come? Isn't it time to vote for the candidate who has come across to us as the one most likely to think of himself as the "education" governor and then become exactly that? One four-year span (or eight) is not going to be enough time to accomplish the awesome task of pulling ourselves up by our educational brogans, but now's the time for greatly revived efforts. We're obliged to vote our heads and our hearts rather than our pocketbooks. It's considered suicidal in Kentucky politics to acknowledge forthrightly the need for more taxes; therefore, most candidates handle this issue as if it were the original poisoned apple cooked to order by the wicked witch.

If we can watch the price of a diet cola (totally lacking in nutrient value) rise from five cents to fifty-five cents and seventy cents and scarcely blink an eye, why do we become so miserly and suspicious when it comes to funding the one thing that pleads to be the most precious of all as we move from the sunrise to the sunset of our lives? Maybe somebody will say, well, it's exactly because the price of everything from candy bars to chewing gum to back scratchers has doubled, tripled, quadrupled and sometimes double-quadrupled that we have to be so careful how we spend our educational dollars. Aren't we putting a lot of junk food and gimcracks ahead of those things that of necessity should be nourishing our minds and activating our bodies? And isn't that a crying shame? If we sacrifice two junk edibles or two of the most worthless thingamabobs every day for the next four years we will have accumulated more than four billion dollars.

Then we might say to the new governor, this is our four billion dollars and we insist that you do everything within your power to see that this money that we have made sacrifices to raise goes into making education in Kentucky among the very finest in the nation.

*David*

# PIECES OF PAPER, INDIVIDUAL INTEGRITY

*I*t's probably best to think of any election, especially a presidential contest, as merely a point in time for the electorate, quite apart from the bitterness of defeat for the loser or the sweetness of victory for the winner. We all lose some, and we all gain some–the problems and the demands are still there just as they were before the election. So are the campaign promises, many of which will soon be falling like leaves in the sweet evening breeze.

The same is true of the issues. Here in Kentucky the lottery, casinos, "charitable gambling," and the broad-form deed are no less controversial, no less debatable, and no less subject to possible litigation. The outcome of any election is neither magic wand nor sledgehammer. The political process continues with a different cast of characters. The constant resides–as it always has and always will–with the individual citizen and the aggregation of communities within the Commonwealth. This does not nullify election results or the immediate resolution of issues. It addresses the greater truth that life is not represented by destinations nearly so well as by the journeys taken one step at a time.

The importance of individual courage and conviction cannot be overstated. In his presidential campaign speech of October 22, 1928, candidate Herbert Hoover invoked "the American system of rugged individualism." He had no idea how rugged it was about to become. Two years later, I was a child of the Great Depression, a little boy who, at the age of eighteen months, lost his father. I survived with nothing more than dirt on my knees and the end of my nose. There's a picture of me sitting on a balcony in Cincinnati, diapers dirty and face smeared with big city soot. All I possessed was a developing brain and something called "the innate aspect of behavior that is unlearned, complex and normally adaptive"–God-given instinct.

Mr. Hoover called Prohibition "a great social and economic experiment, noble in motive and far-reaching in purpose." I, who was born with some sense of my own, would later learn that possibly as many lives were ruined during Prohibition as before and after it. As an issue and as an amendment to the Constitution, its passage was one of those points in time in the adult world, both in its ratification and in its repeal. Meantime, I, the child, managed just fine with dirt on my knees and the end of my nose.

The same thing is true of gambling and the broad-form deed. Pieces of paper are hardly justifications for overhauling our ethical engines. Just because there's a lottery in Ohio doesn't mean someone should cross the river to purchase a ticket. Just because there's a place to buy a lottery ticket on the way to work in Kentucky doesn't mean someone should rob a piggy bank for such a purchase. Just because there's a gambling boat docked on the north bank of the Ohio River doesn't mean there should be land-based casinos throughout the Commonwealth of Kentucky. Just because there is permission to tear up a mountain doesn't mean someone should buy stock in bulldozers.

The Commonwealth needs more people willing to stand up on their hind legs and say, "Hell, no." That's the kind of Kentuckian who fought for and won "The Dark and Bloody Ground." It was another piece of paper, the proclamation of 1763, issued by George III, that attempted to draw a line along the Appalachian Mountains over which American pioneers were "forbidden" to cross. But cross they did, especially after passage of the Hard Labor Treaty of 1768. Kentucky historian laureate Thomas D. Clark describes it in his *History of Kentucky*: "Adventurous men came westward walking at the head and rear of processions, driving cattle, sheep, and hogs. Women and children formed the center, driving pack horses loaded with household necessities, and perhaps, bits of eastern finery with which feminine hearts were loath to part."

Legal documents and approved legislation are necessary in all societies claiming to be civilized, and this is no advocacy or apologia for scofflaw behavior. When individuals wait for paper endorsements of what they instinctively believe to be true, then they're selling their birthrights–wrong at any price.

With the New Guy headed for the White House, and the other election day questions settled for now, it's time for individuals to look within themselves for the most truthful answers of all. There is a moral law, a moral obligation, a moral certainty, and a moral victory. They are achieved every day of every individual's life.

*David*

# FINAL CURTAIN

$\mathcal{M}$adison County has Cassius Marcellus Clay. Now it has Wally.

The two of them belong to the ages–Clay, the fire-eating nineteenth-century abolitionist, Wallace "Wally" Neal Briggs, the twentieth-century actor, director, and author of *Riverside Remembered*. Both lie asleep on a knoll in the Richmond Cemetery, yet both will be with us in the twenty-first century–Clay to remind us that slavery in all its ugly forms is an abomination, Wally to keep us smiling and singing and never taking ourselves too seriously.

When he was buried in the summer of 1993, not far from the old emancipationist, the day was hot and Wally would have said, "Take your coats off, for goodness sakes."

They used to kid Wally about his ears being so big. But Wally wore his big ears like badges of honor. He was an immaculate dresser–collar double-starched and pinched, tie precisely in place, hair combed with no strand gone astray, shoes shined to Marine Corps perfection. My wife, Lalie, who loved Wally very much, noticed that the mortician had had a little trouble with the tying of the ascot. So she hovered over the casket and fixed it the way he would have done it. Oh, Wally could be rumpled when he wanted to be. He was very rumpled when he played Harvey. Wally was the rabbit, and audiences loved him for it.

He was casually dressed when he returned to the theater in the evenings for the productions he directed. There were so many over the years: *Street Scene, The Diary of Anne Frank, Cyrano de Bergerac, Twelfth Night, The Taming of the Shrew, Mister Roberts*. Wally could be very intense. He could move in close to an actor's face and say, "That's it! That's it! Now BUILD on it!!!" Or, as in *Country Girl*, which he directed and in which he played the leading role, he could say to me, "Here, let me show you how to kiss her!"

Near the end of his lovely life, I encouraged him to complete the book that had lain like a thick and dog-eared manuscript for so long. Wally had wanted to call it *Down by Riverside*, but he allowed his publisher, the University Press of Kentucky, to retitle it *Riverside Remembered*, the touching, magnolia-sweet story of Wally's old home place in Mississippi, the story of "Buster" growing up in the Deep South.

Yes, there was a cast party following the graveside services for Wally. Ann Robinson, one of the actresses in *Street Scene*, made her baby grand reverberate with the sounds of the music Wally had loved. Cyrano–the late Bill Nave–was there to sing his heart out, and I, Ensign Pulver, clumsily, tonelessly hummed along, Ensign Pulver who had had so much difficulty with the closing line in Mister Roberts. Wally had coached me to say, finally, "Mr. Roberts is dead." Wally's words are as alive today as they were a long time ago: "Just say it, Dave, just say it: 'Mr. Roberts is dead.'" Wally had worked very hard with Pulver to deliver the line, simply and clearly. "Just say it flat out," he patiently instructed. "Don't exaggerate it, don't emphasize any of the words, just say it low and straight and let the words come out of your mouth, even and smooth without trying to be dramatic: 'Mr. Roberts is dead'."

Wally had been very proud that night, as he was at all the other performances. After he had given a production every ounce of energy from his total being, at dress rehearsal he would sit on the back row in the theater and draw the production into his arms like a prodigal child come home. He would laugh and he would cry. He would applaud as if the student actors had pleased him to the center of his soul.

The eulogy for Wally had been just right. There was laughter and there were poorly disguised tears. And then there was the ride down Interstate 75, across Clay's Ferry Bridge, home to Madison County. Wally wouldn't be going home to Mississippi. He'd be going to be with his beloved wife,

Olive, who'd been waiting for him on the knoll overlooking Richmond.

The procession passed the final resting place of Cassius Marcellus Clay, then stopped where the ground was freshly turned. After the brief services, a woman's voice, my wife's, began to sing, softly, barely audibly. "There's No Business Like Show Business." Lalie hoped others would join her and that the cast party would begin immediately, but they didn't, and the words were left to float across the knoll, smoothly, undramatically, like a mysterious wisp of a breeze on a day hot with sorrow.

Wally must've loved it.

*David*

# HOLDING FAST

$\mathcal{T}$he splendid thing about the Dinsmore Homestead in Boone County is that James Dinsmore could walk in today and find it looking much the way it did when he and his family lived there in 1842.

True, more than a century ago, Mr. Dinsmore (1790-1872) passed on, but the house he built stands just as it used to be on what is today KY 18, about six and a half miles west of Burlington. (Take Exit 181 from I-75 at Florence.) It's a winding, peaceful drive, a glorious opportunity to celebrate the advent of spring after the passage of another winter. Consider it a thought to warm a February day!

The Dinsmore Homestead Foundation is committed to perpetuating in 1999 and on into the twenty-first century the memory of a family. It's living proof that despite Thomas Wolfe's dire belief to the contrary, you can go home again and probably should.

Five generations of the Dinsmore family lived (1842-1988) in the two-story house graciously accessible to the public today. The steps are sturdy that lead upward from the second floor to the attic, meant to pass most any test of time, the attic where children may have explored, dreaming of many exotic, antebellum places. Old trunks with their mysterious contents rest in their own eternities, and a visitor can stand there and wonder about it.

There's a parlor, certainly, and since most homes at the end of the twentieth century don't have such old fashioned things as parlors (what my country preacher grandfather used to call "the room of honor of state–woe to the family that has no best room–the Lord's day is the parlour of the week") a visitor to the Dinsmore Homestead can savor the feeling of standing in a rural nineteenth-century Kentucky parlor.

A James Dinsmore portrait hangs over the mantelpiece, patriarchal head unapologetically bald, beard full, nose prominently Roman, eyes soft yet resolute, lips closed concealing a likely economy of words. James married Martha Macomb, and they had three daughters, Isabella, Julia, and Susan. Only Isabella married (Charles Flandrau), and they had two daughters, raised by their Aunt Julia.

It was Julia Dinsmore who inherited the farm in 1872 and operated it for the next fifty-four years. Until the day she died in 1926, Julia kept a diary, setting an example for all of us. Last November, while making a presentation to a workshop of genealogists at the Dinsmore House, I talked about journal keeping as a vital human activity. It brought the following response by some of those present:

"It increased my sense of the need for documenting daily thoughts and impressions...a broader concept of how everything around you is part of your history."

The African-American Heritage Task Force of Northern Kentucky has expressed an interest in Dinsmore Homestead documents, numbering almost 90,000 pages, for it is no secret that James Dinsmore was a slave owner, although not a Simon Legree (the major villain in Harriet Beecher Stowe's *Uncle Tom's Cabin*). One free African-American nursemaid, Julia Loving, lived with the Dinsmore family. She had a brother, Walter, who had a natural talent for music. Although the sister at first discouraged his trumpet playing, Julia Dinsmore was recorded as having said: "Let the boy play!" Well, play he did. Walter Loving attended the New England School of Music and did graduate work in Leipzig, becoming well known throughout the United States.

A possible New Year's lesson from the Dinsmore Homestead: preserve that which is right, change that which is wrong; hold fast and build up rather than tear down.

*David*

# JOURNAL KEEPING

*J*ournal keeping, not unlike housekeeping, is a vanishing art. It speaks to the times in which we live–so much hustling and bustling there seems not to be time for some simpler activity. I kept a daily journal for about twenty years, and it became such a vital part of my life it became almost imperative that I make the entries. No one was looking over my shoulder except myself. No one was evaluating what I wrote, because I never cared one whit what others thought about it. The freedom of expression was almost indescribable. Yet I was writing for others, reasoning that it would be satisfying and perhaps important to leave a record for unborn generations. I could feel the warm breath of immortality as I imagined my journal read aloud by the fireplace on a cold winter's night in home sweet Kentucky.

"Daddy, let's read great-grandfather tonight."

"You mean you don't want to watch the coverage of the landing on Jupiter?"

"Gee, Dad, we saw that live this afternoon at school and, anyway, it wasn't all that different from the landing on Mars."

"Well, all right, but I hope somebody remembered to record it so I can watch it later."

"Gotcha covered, Dad. Now, about great-grandfather. Let's go back to the late twentieth century."

"Pick a year."

"How about 1982? Wasn't that the year he was tramping all over the place? Central America, South America, the Middle East?"

"O.K., let's see if we can find 1982. Here we are. We've got to do something about the binding on these things one of these days. Mother, would you pour me a little brandy while I add another log to the fire?"

"Dad, how come we still use a fireplace, since all the other kids live in houses heated with solar energy?"

"Oh, I don't know, maybe it's a throwback to those olden days. Maybe it's keeping touch. There's so much solar energy it's kind of nice to be primitive once in a while."

"You're a real sucker for that old stuff, aren't you, Dad?"

"Never mind that. You asked for 1982, and 1982 is what you're going to get. Your great-grandfather was reporting the war in El Salvador for CBS News."

I miss you. Pray for me. And join me in prayer for the 560 children I saw today at the refugee camp in Santa Tecla. Can you imagine: A total of 1,000 people living on one acre of land? And you and I have 106 acres for the two of us. Until you have seen such a place you cannot possibly know the hurt I felt. And I think that those of us who are so wealthy must know about these things so close to our doorstep. It is numbing, just numbing to see these dirty, hungry, crowded children–to see the sad, withered faces of the old men and women who have managed to survive another day of this sad, withering civil war. The shortage of water, the grinding of corn, the gruel for the babies–and those faces, oh, those heart-rending faces. Damn it, can't the killing stop? Can't the hungry be fed: I will never forget this day as long as I live.

I wrote and recorded a spot for radio and then returned with the crew, Mario and Shlomo, our interpreter, Viviana, and our driver to the hotel. As soon as we arrived we were turned back and sent to San Sebastion, because there had been reports of another firefight there. When we arrived, we learned that that was not the case, but we did get footage of a funeral procession, the tolling of the bell in the church tower where on Sunday a guerrilla had gained entry and had fired on the town...we taped the grieving people in the church...and nearby, the ashes of a guerrilla that had been burned.

For a time, it seemed more fighting might begin, but it was as if echoes from Sunday were reverberating. We hurried back to San Salvador. I fed the World Tonight and then wrote and helped edit a piece for Morning. I had a late club sandwich in the hotel coffee shop. I love you, Lalie, and want you in my arms.

"Lalie is your great-grandmother."
"You mean, grandmother Ravy's mother?"
"Yes."

*David*